Spitfire!

Spitfire!

The Experiences of a Battle of Britain Fighter Pilot

BRIAN LANE

Edited by
Dilip Sarkar MBE FRHistS

AMBERLEY

This edition first published 2011

Amberley Publishing
The Hill, Stroud
Gloucestershire, GL5 4EP

www.amberleybooks.com

Copyright © Brian Lane, 1942, 2009, 2011
Copyright © edited edition, Dilip Sarkar, 2009, 2011

British Library Cataloguing in Publication Data.
A catalogue record for this book is available from the British Library.

ISBN 978 1 84868 354 9

Typesetting and Origination by Amberley Publishing
Printed in Great Britain.

CONTENTS

Foreword by Dilip Sarkar

During the Second World War, the general public's demand for information about the conflict, especially as experienced first-hand by fighting men, was insatiable. This led to the publication of innumerable related books and articles, all intended as morale boosting tales of derring-do, and none were more popular than accounts written by fighter pilots - Spitfire pilots in particular. The Supermarine Spitfire, designed by R.J. Mitchell and at first built in Southampton, was, of course, everyone's favourite: the elliptical wing, sleek lines and the roar of the mighty Rolls Royce Merlin engine made up a potent brew indeed. The Spitfire became the very physical embodiment of freedom and defiance, and those who flew her were revered; as Flight Lieutenant Ken Wilkinson, once said to me 'If you were a fighter pilot you were a cocky so-and-so, top button undone and all that, but if you were a *Spitfire* pilot then you were cockier still, a definite cut above the rest!'

Amongst this plethora of inspirational literature was a small work entitled *Spitfire!*, by Squadron Leader B.J. Ellan DFC. Written from scribbled diary notes and log book entries, *Spitfire!* provides a rare insight into the events of our Finest Hour, as experienced by those young fighter pilots on the front line. To those men, many of whom were only in their early 20s, violent and sudden death was omnipresent, and they lived life literally one day at a time – but with an intense zest and enthusiasm. When he wrote *Spitfire!*, shortly after the momentous events of 1940, but whilst Britain was still very much at war, the author was unaffected by the later historiography of doubts and controversies that began to, and still do, revolve around the Battle of Britain. That is what makes *Spitfire!* so special, written as it was in those almost innocent circumstances, by a 23 year old, who simply told the story of the fighting over Dunkirk and subsequent Battle of Britain, as experienced by himself and fellow pilots.

Who was the author? Well, he was certainly not, in fact, 'B.J. Ellan', which was a pseudonym chosen by the wartime censor, but actually Squadron Leader Brian James Edward Lane DFC. Indeed, the censor preserved not only the author's anonymity, but equally that of other RAF personnel and bases mentioned in the book. In place of such identifying detail, the original edition, published in 1942, were simply blanks or clues, such as 'F/Sgt U' and 'aerodrome at M'. This, to me, made the work even more fascinating, inspiring me over 20 years ago to embark upon literally a detective inquiry to put names and places to the censor's blanks. So it was that 'F/ Sgt U' became Flight Sergeant George Cecil Unwin DFM, one of Fighter Command's most successful and aggressive fighter pilots in 1940, and the 'aerodrome at M' was identified as Manston in Kent. Slowly but surely, essentially using contemporary RAF records, such as squadron diaries and the combat reports of individual pilots, almost all the blanks were filled in (a handful of elusive individuals are marked as such in the text), and a detailed and vibrant picture emerged of Brian Lane and his fellow pilots of 19 Squadron during our so-called 'Finest Hour'. Moreover, my quest took me to all points of the compass to actually meet and, as it turned out, befriend many of these personalities from the pages of history – to Ferndown where I found Wing Commander Unwin DSO DFM, Southampton to find 'Sgt J' – Wing Commander Bernard Jennings AFC, Reading to meet one of the two 'Sgt Cs' – Wing Commander David Cox DFC (sadly the other, Sergeant 'Chaz' Charnock, did not survive the war), and to Salisbury where I met 'G' – Wing Commander Gordon Sinclair; 'Frankie' – Flying Officer Frank Brinsden – even travelled to England from New Zealand to meet me! From Australia, Air Commodore James Coward wrote to me of his Battle of Britain experiences, and interview notes and letters from all involved rapidly represented a substantial archive of memories. This new edition of 'Spitfire!' is, therefore, unique, given that my research from all those years ago means that there are no censor's blanks to puzzle the reader – instead we have inserted every identity and place name, making this a comprehensively informed, whilst retaining the authenticity and atmosphere of Brian Lane's original classic.

Brian Lane came from Pinner in Middlesex. A former pupil of St Paul's who, having been sacked from his job in a light bulb producing factory, was accepted for a Short Service Commission in the RAF during 1936. He joined his first fighter squadron, No 66, flying Gauntlet biplanes at Duxford, in 1937, before joining 213 Squadron, with whom he converted to Hawker Hurricanes in 1938. Later that year he suffered a flying accident en route to leave in London, and then, after recuperation, joined No 19 Squadron at Duxford as Commander of 'A' Flight. No 19 was one of the RAF's premier fighter squadrons, with a long and proud history, and in August 1938, had become the service's first unit to equip with the new Spitfire.

On 26 May 1940, 19 Squadron's Commanding Officer, Squadron Leader Geoffrey Stephenson, was shot down and captured during the Squadron's first full-formation combat over Dunkirk. It thereafter fell to Flight Lieutenant Lane to lead the Squadron, both in the air and on the ground, but permanent command did not pass to him: after Operation DYNAMO an 'outsider', Squadron Leader Phillip Pinkham AFC, was appointed CO of 19 Squadron. Although many personnel felt that Brian Lane should have got the Squadron, typically Lane himself merely ensured that the new CO was given every support and loyalty. For his efforts during DYNAMO, however, Brian Lane was awarded a much deserved Distinguished Flying Cross, and his official rating as a fighter pilot was 'exceptional'.

At this time the Squadron was evaluating the experimental cannon-armed Spitfire Mk IB, which was proving extremely troublesome due to stoppages and jamming. Whilst Squadron Leader Pinkham busied himself with resolving this problem, Flight

Lieutenant Lane continued to lead the Squadron into action. On 5 September 1940, however, whilst the Battle of Britain was reaching its peak, Squadron Leader Pinkham was shot down by a Me 109 over Kent and killed on his first combat sortie. Common sense, and not the pre-war pecking order, then prevailed and Brian Lane, by now an extremely experienced combat pilot, was at last promoted to squadron leader and given command of 19 Squadron. Having already led the Squadron throughout much of the Battle of Britain, Squadron Leader Lane continued to do so, 19 Squadron operating from Fowlmere Farm, in the Duxford Sector, as part of the controversial 'Big Wing' led by Squadron Leader Douglas Bader, the legendary, legless, CO of 242 Squadron.

After the Battle of Britain, Brian Lane survived being shot down by a Hurricane, flown by the CO of a North Weald Hurricane squadron, and continued flying on operations until June 1941, when he was posted away on a staff appointment to the Middle East. Some of his former pilots on 19 Squadron remember him: - Flight Sergeant George 'Grumpy' Unwin DFM: 'Although Brian was an officer and I was an NCO, and therefore segregated on the ground, we were friends. We were in complete accord in the air. He was completely unflappable, no matter what the odds, his voice always calm and reassuring, issuing orders which always seemed to be the right decisions'.

Flying Officer Frank 'Fanny' Brinsden: 'Brian was always so much more sophisticated than the rest of us, I remember that he used a silver cigarette case, but without affectation, and his wife, Eileen, was a famous pre-war racing driver – some achievement for a female in those days!'

Sergeant David Cox: 'Quite simply Brian Lane was the best CO I ever served under, in every respect, and when my turn came to lead I modelled myself on him. He always seemed to know and remember just about everything about everyone.'

Corporal Fred Roberts: 'I looked after the guns on Squadron Leader Lane's Spitfire, and he was an absolutely wonderful man.

Early on in the war, some of the officers could still be a bit snobbish, but not Brian Lane, who knew everyone in his command, no matter how lowly their rank or status, by their first names.'

An 'ace' fighter pilot and inspirational leader, his staff appointment suggests that Brian Lane's great potential had been recognised. Unfortunately he found the climate disagreeable, so was sent back to the UK in September 1942, and began a Spitfire refresher course at Rednal in Shropshire. Three months later, Squadron Leader Lane joined 167 'Gold Coast' Squadron as a supernumerary squadron leader, to gain up-to-date operational experience before given another command. No 167, a Dutch squadron, was based at Ludham in Norfolk, flying the outdated Spitfire Mk V, which had been outclassed by the FW 190 in every respect. Indeed, the 190, had massively reduced the Spitfire's depth of penetration over enemy occupied Europe and dominated the day fighter war until introduction of the improved Spitfire Mk IX, which swung the balance back in the RAF's favour.

On 13 December 1942, Squadron Leader Lane made his first flight from Ludham, a local familiarisation flight. That afternoon, he led a section of Spitfires low over the North Sea on a 'Rhubarb', a low-level sweep over the Dutch coast, looking for targets of opportunity. Nothing of any interest was seen, however, but as the Spitfires prepared to retire, two FW 190s appeared. Squadron Leader Lane, whose radio was unserviceable, turned to attack and was last seen chasing a 190 inland. The other Spitfires made it home safely, but 167 Squadron waited in vain for Squadron Leader Lane's return: the 25-year old was reported 'Missing in Action'. Years later my researches indicated that an FW 190 pilot, *Oberleutnant* Walter Leonhardt of 2/JG 1, claimed to have destroyed a Spitfire over the North Sea, 20 miles west of Schouen Island: Lane's was the only Spitfire lost that day. The final moments of Brian Lane's gallant life are easy to imagine: his pursuit of the 190 was futile in a Spitfire Mk V, the 190 able to always keep ahead; with fuel reserves a priority when operating so far across the water eventually the Spitfire pilot would have to break off and head for England. At that point the 190 clearly reversed the tables, hunter becoming the hunted, until catching and destroying the lone RAF fighter over the cold and inhospitable North Sea, which became Brian Lane's only shroud and last resting place.

The postscript to this story is that on 2 February 1943, *Oberleutnant* Leonhardt was shot down over the North Sea in combat with American Liberator bombers, 60 miles north west of Texel; like Squadron Leader Lane DFC, he has no known grave. Leonhardt himself was an intelligent and fit young man, and, also like Brian Lane, was a successful fighter pilot; both young men clearly had great potential for the future, more importantly in peacetime, perhaps, and so their losses really emphasise what a massive waste of young life war is. Moreover, for an officer of Brian Lane's experience to be lost on such a completely pointless sortie was criminal; many pilots recognised that 'Rhubarbs' were pointless, but they continued, the casualties racking up, until the Kenley Wing Leader, Wing Commander Johnnie Johnson, made representation whilst on a staff appointment between tours in 1943. Sadly, this was too late to save Brian Lane, author of *Spitfire! Experiences of a Fighter Pilot*, and many others like him.

In addition to being a first-hand account of a Spitfire pilot's experience during 1940, *Spitfire!* also provides a contemporary social comment. For example, the author mentions the Squadron's groundcrews 'working like niggers', a comment that would, quite rightly, be completely unacceptable in today's multi-racial and enlightened society. It is also unlikely that phrases such as 'the mindless Hun' would be used today, but, of course, when *Spitfire!* was written – not by a journalist but by a 23 year old fighter pilot – Britain was engaged in armed conflict with Nazi Germany – a struggle that could only end in total defeat for one or the other power.

Dilip Sarkar MBE FRHistS, 9 April 2009

Dramatis Personae

The identities of the author and other personnel mentioned in 'Spitfire!' were originally censored, but this list identifies those concerned for the reader.

S/Ldr BJ Ellan	Squadron Leader B.J.E. Lane (19 Sqn)
'EJ'	S/L E.J. Edwardes-Jones, a C.O. of 213 Sqn
'Mac'	Squadron Leader Eric McNab, a C.O. of 213 Sqn
Wilf	Flight Lieutenant W.G. Clouston (19 Sqn)
F/Sgt S	Flight Sergeant Harry Steere (19 Sqn)
John	Flying Officer G.W. 'Johnnie' Petre (19 Sqn)
Michael	Pilot Officer M.D. Lyne (19 Sqn)
S/Ldr L	Squadron Leader James 'Prof' Leathart (54 Sqn)
F/Sgt U	Flight Sergeant G.C. 'Grumpy' Unwin (19 Sqn)
Eric/'B'	Flying Officer Eric Ball (19 Sqn)
Watty	Pilot Officer P.V. Watson (19 Sqn)
Sgt P	Sargeant Jack Potter (19 Sqn)
'G'	Flying Officer Gordon Sinclair (19 Sqn)
Sgt J	Sargeant Bernard 'Jimmy' Jennings (19 Sqn)
S/Ldr M	Squadron Leader 'Tubby' Mermagen (222 Sqn)
'Cras'	Flying Officer J.H.E. Crastor (Intelligence Officer, 19 Sqn)
Leonard	Flying Officer L.A. 'Ace' Haines (19 Sqn)
Woody	Wing Commander 'Woody' Woodhall, Station Commander, Duxford
S/Ldr P	Squadron Leader Phillip 'Tommy' Pinkham (19 Sqn)
Frankie	F/O F.N. Brinsden
Jock	Pilot Officer Wallace Cunningham (19 Sqn)
'F'	Flight Lieutenant Walter 'Farmer' Lawson (19 Sqn)

Sgt P (Czech)	Sargeant Plzak (19 Sqn)
Russell	Flying Officer J.R. Budd (Adjutant, 19 Sqn)
S/Ldr B	Squadron Leader D.R.S. Bader (242 Sqn)
Dolly (Czech)	Pilot Officer F. Dolezal (19 Sqn)
'The Admiral'	Sub-Lieutenant Giles Blake, FAA (19 Sqn)
Sgt R	Sargeant Roden (19 Sqn)
Sgt C	Sargeant D.G.S.R. Cox & Sgt H.C. Charnock (60th 19 Sqn)
'H' (Czech)	Pilot Officer Hradil (19 Sqn)
Arthur	Pilot Officer Arthur Vokes (19 Sqn)
'L'	S/L Lionel Gaunce C.O. of 249 Sqn

Locations

'new squadron forming at N'	No 266 Squadron at Northolt
Aerodrome M	Manston, Kent
Beach at D	Deal, Kent
Airfield at R	Rochford, Essex
Airfield at C	Coltishall, Norfolk
Airfield at H	Hornchurch, Essex
Elementary Flying Training School at H	Hamble

Abbreviations

A.A.	Ack Ack or anti-aircraft fire
R/T	Radio telephone
E/A	Enemy aircraft
F.T.S.	Flying Training School
S/L	Squadron Leader
C.O.	Commanding Officer
F/O	Flying Officer
W/C	Wing Commander
Sgt	Sergeant
F/Sgt	Flight Sergeant
F/L	Flight Lieutenant

Author's Note

The title of this book no doubt tells you what it is about. The name "Spitfire" first became a household word during the "Blitz" of last year, but before this these wonderful aircraft had given us valiant service at Dunkirk.

In this book I have set down the experiences of a pilot in a fighter squadron - myself. I have been with the squadron since the beginning of the war, first as a flight commander and later as C.O., and I never wish to meet a grander bunch of blokes. We went all through Dunkirk and the "Blitz" which followed a couple of months later, and in telling my story I have tried to answer the question of the man in the street: "What is it like up there?" and to give you an idea of what a fighter pilot feels and thinks as he fights up there in the blue.

To any members of the squadron who may read this book, I hope I have not left out any of their pet exploits, but if I have I hope they will bear with me and remember that I have had to write in odd moments after "release," etc., and under the difficulty of carrying on with the job in hand at the same time. "So few," Mr. Churchill said—but no debt here as he would have you believe; rather few so lucky to be able to get on with the job whilst less fortunate folk looked on and awaited their chance. I think he was really referring to our mess bills, anyway!

In conclusion, I should like to pay tribute to the men who design and build our fighting aircraft: Our successes are their successes, for it is they who have placed in our hands the finest aircraft and equipment in the world. To them we owe a special debt of gratitude.

How to Shoot a Line

Shooting a line doesn't necessarily refer to shooting Huns, although sometimes it is much the same thing! By writing this book I am *shooting a line*, in other words, talking about myself, and what I have done. Usually, however, a line is a semi-deliberate exaggeration of a humorous nature—a tall story about yourself, if you like. If you write a book or get your name in the paper that is a *ginormous* line, the strange word being' evolved from gigantic and enormous.

Some people *shoot lines* unconsciously all the time, that is, they swank, and everybody soon becomes *browned off* with them, i.e., fed up. The lad who swanks is looked upon as a *poor type*, whilst a popular chap is a *good type*. There is a lot more general slang, but I won't trouble you with it since you won't find it in the chapters which follow. Instead, I'll deal with the technical terms which may prove difficult to understand.

First take the aerodrome. This is occasionally referred to as *the drome*, but more usually as *the deck*. *Deck* also means terra firma in general. As opposed to dry land, the sea is called *the drink*.

The correct term for an aeroplane is an *aircraft*, or in slang a kite. To run over *the kite*, first let's take the undercarriage, invariably referred to as *the undercart*. Then there are the *flaps*, which are hinged portions of the wing near the *trailing (rear) edge*, which act as air brakes and reduce the landing speed of the aircraft.

An aircraft *stalls* when it has insufficient forward speed for the wings to maintain their *lift*. If you skim a flat stone over the water, it skims until its speed drops and then sinks or *stalls*. It is very much the same with an aircraft. The *flaps* reduce the *stalling* speed. For instance, a Spitfire stalls with flaps up at 69 m.p.h., and with flaps down at 63 m.p.h. Not an awful lot of difference, you may think, but it makes a world of difference in landing, and you would never get into a small aerodrome if you didn't use the flaps.

I have used the word *wings* several times above, but the technical term is *mainplanes,* as opposed to the *tailplane*. The cockpit is called the *office,* and the control column just the *stick. Rudder bars* refers to the trimming tab on the rudder. By winding the *bias control* one way or the other moves the tab and gives port or starboard bias. The *elevators* on the *tailplane* have a similar device on them. These are necessary, as the *trim* of an aircraft varies with its speed and altitude. The *trimmers* relieve the pilot of the strain of pressing on the *stick* or rudder bar all the time.

Another thing you'll find in the *office* is the *R/T* control. *R/T* is the wireless equipment, consisting of a transmitter and receiver with a three-way switch control, Transmit—Off—Receive.

Now let's take off. Once *airborne,* i.e., off the ground, you *retract the undercart,* shut the *lid,* i.e., close the hood, and put the *prop* or *fan* into coarse pitch, which on an aircraft is much the same thing as changing gear on a car. (By the way, the *prop* is never called a propeller. The correct term is *airscrew* if you don't use the slang words.)

Now supposing you meet some Huns and manage to get on the tail of one of them. If he isn't a very experienced pilot, or if the machine is not very maneuverable or well armed, he is *easy meat* or *cold meat*. You press the firing button and *give him a squirt.*

If you are unlucky enough to get shot down yourself, you *bale out, step out,* or *take to the silk*. If you land *in the drink* you are wearing a *Mae West,* which is a lifesaving waistcoat which gives you curves in the right places! A parachute is called a *brolly* or a *jumpsack.*

Well, now you know, and if I were to say that I nearly lost my prop to-day, I wouldn't mean that it fell off, but that I nearly stalled (stopped) the engine, which would have been a bad show, wouldn't' it ?

Chapter 1
Luck:
1935-August 1939

I am told that I was born with a silver spoon in my mouth, which they say is a sign of luck. I have certainly been lucky all my life.

When the Hun was plagued with his vile disease a generation ago I could not lend a hand to cure him, my sole activity in this direction being when my nurse showed me what she called a Zeppelin and I blew a very immature raspberry at it. It was probably just one of our own blimps, at that.

In 1939, when the plague seized Europe again, I had another tale to tell. My luck was in.

But first of all I must go back a bit to the year 1935, when my story really begins. I was then employed by a big electrical firm, my job being to supervise a dozen or so girls turning out hundreds of electric bulbs. Quite a responsible position for an eighteen-year-old. It was always rather a mystery to me how I got it! However, the experience stood me in good stead. I learned a lot about human nature (and women!) if not much about the manufacture of lamps.

I was not really surprised when one day the powers-that-be informed me that the period of my employment coincided with a decline in their profits, and that if I would kindly leave them they could get along better without me. I complied with this request and went home to my lamenting parents with the additional news that I wanted to try for the R.A.F., which was then in course of expansion.

To want was one thing, to get there another. I filled in and sent off form after form, asking every conceivable sort of question, and then sat back and waited. Nothing happened for a bit, so I started to make a nuisance of myself at Adastral House. So that they shouldn't forget me there I paid such frequent visits that the sergeant at the door began to greet me like an old friend and was always ready with a facetious remark.

But at last I received a notification to report to the Selection Board. I imagine a microbe on a slide under a microscope feels much the same way as I did before the Board, but apparently they liked the look of me, for they passed me on to the doctors. A week after came a letter to say I had been accepted and telling me to report to the Elementary Flying School at Hamble.

Then followed two months of bliss for me but not for my instructor, a gentle giant with the most amazing capacity for beer of anyone I have ever met. He could drink any two men under the table with ease, but no matter how much beer he absorbed, it never seemed to have the least effect on him. He always turned up bright and cheerful in the morning, which was more than I could say for myself sometimes, and nothing ever seemed to disturb him—not even my flying! I remember once going up with him to do aerobatics. He started to show me a slow roll, when half-way through came a muffled oath down the speaking tube and the aircraft did a most amazing manœuvre, coming out right way up. I heard my instructor laugh, and then he said, "I've forgotten to do up my ruddy straps!"

Shortly after I went solo my luck was on one occasion hard put to it to save me, but it held. I was doing circuits and bumps and feeling like a young god, as one does at this period of training, when I was rudely disturbed by the terrifying sight of another aircraft heading straight at me, mere yards away. I never stop being amazed at the speed at which the human brain can work in an emergency, and somehow I and the other pilot just about avoided the fatal collision. I say just about, because we did hit each other, the undercarriage of my kite knocking most of the other chap's rudder off. If there had been two instructors in the aircraft instead of two beginners, they would both have been killed for sure, but God looks after drunks and fools, and we lived to fly another day.

The instructors were very kind to us about this incident. Apart from telling us to say our prayers twice that night they left it at that. My own instructor, who was away at the time, merely remarked when he returned that he always missed all the fun! The most long-suffering folk in the world, instructors, and the finest psychologists. A harsh word or a raspberry at the time would probably have upset our nerves.

After two months we completed the course, and with fifty hours flying to each pupil's credit, twenty-five solo and twenty-five dual, we were sent to a Service Flying Training School at Wittering to complete our training on Service type aircraft.

Here, again we found the finest instructors and training in the world, and we were passed out and posted to squadrons. I had applied to go to a fighter squadron, and had been trained on Furies to this end, so I was tremendously pleased when I found I had been posted to a Gauntlet squadron, the Gauntlet being the latest fighter in the Service and one of the most wonderful aircraft ever built. It was almost the last of the biplane fighters and a perfect joy to handle.

Some months with this squadron, during which time I received training in operational flying, and then I answered the call for volunteers to go to a new squadron, No. 266, which was forming at Northolt. The first person I saw when I arrived there was an old school friend, Jackie Sing, who had been at St. Paul's with me. He was to be my flight commander for the two and a half happy years I spent with the squadron. Our first C.O. was Eric McNab, a Canadian and one of the best, who was one of the finest pilots in the Service. He later took over one of the flights and S/L E.J. Edwardes-Jones, pre-war C.O. of

213 squadron succeeded him. I am sure we were the happiest squadron going, for S/L E.J. Edwardes-Jones was a perfect C.O. I never heard him annoyed with anyone, and he never needed to be, for we would all do anything for him and in addition he had a fine sense of humour which never deserted him.

Time passed, and after the crisis of September, 1938, the squadron was re-equipped with Hurricanes. A grand kite, the Hurricane, and one which was to do magnificent service in the near future. March, 1939, came and went. Mussolini took Albania. August, and the drums of war were beating. Hitler screamed his piece over Danzig, and then it came—War! Now in their true perspective we saw. those years of training and flying, that unending stream of new pilots, those mock war operations—they were not just a game or the means of a livelihood, but experience now to be tested to the utmost in the grim new reality of war.

We quickly fell into the new routine, standing by all day and half the night, waiting for a blow that did not come. A few days after war was declared I was posted to my present, squadron as a flight commander, and although I didn't want to leave a very happy squadron, still a change does everyone good and I soon settled down among another grand bunch of blokes this time flying Spitfires.

Chapter 2

First Blood:
September 1939-25 May 1940

It was a queer war. Everybody said so. The experts said it was going to be a war of attrition. Maybe that was their word for it, but it was still a queer war. The Luftwaffe's expected blows on this island did not fall. Goering contented himself instead with raids by single aircraft against the convoys round the coasts. So for month after month we patrolled the shipping, no doubt frightening away many Huns but never so much as catching sight of one.

One day in October, however, excitement ran high in the squadron. "B" Flight were on patrol over a large convoy off the East Coast when the excited voice of Wilf Clouston, the flight commander, came back over the R/T saying he had sighted what he thought must be a raider. He was right, it was a raider, but alas for him the Navy put up a barrage which turned the Hun back and he was cheated of his prey. When the flight came back the remarks of the pilots about the Senior Service were neither respectful nor complimentary!

The winter came on and activity grew less and less. With the spring, however, single Huns began coming over in larger numbers for the purpose of making attacks on shipping or to carry out highflying reconnaissance work. Our luck in "A" Flight seemed to be right out, for it was "B" Flight which drew first blood. On the 11th May, 1940, Wilf with a section of "B" Flight was sent up after a reconnaissance machine over the East Coast. They intercepted him and saw It was a Ju 88 at about 20,000 feet. The section formed line astern and turned into the attack. The Hun saw them coming and put his nose down, going hell for leather towards a layer of cloud at about 5,000 feet. Wilf and F/Sgt Harry Steere each managed to give him a squirt, and then he was into the cloud. A game of hide and seek followed, and Wilf told F/O G.W. 'John' Petre, who was flying No. 3 in the formation, to go beneath the cloud layer in case the Hun should come out below.

As luck would have it, this was what actually happened, and John was able to deliver a good attack, closing to about fifty yards and giving the Hun all he had got. The Hun disappeared in the clouds again and the Spitfires returned to the aerodrome. John came in a few minutes later than the others, touched down and came to rest in the middle of the aerodrome with his engine stopped. We all went out to him to see what was up, and although he personally was all right he had a bullet hole in his oil-tank and several more in the wings and nose. The German rear gunner had put in some good shooting and John had come back from thirty miles out to sea with no oil pressure at all. He had only just managed to make the aerodrome before his engine seized up.

This was the first action in which the squadron was engaged, or as Michael (identity unknown) our Adjutant put it in the Squadron diary, "The first shots to be fired in anger" by the Squadron in the World War of 1939." A few days later came the news that the crew of the Ju 88 had been picked up in the North Sea. The rear gunner claimed to have shot down one Spitfire—he was nearly right!

Just about this time we heard that the squadron was to move to France at short notice, the first Spitfires to be sent overseas. This meant terrific activity for us all in order to be ready for the great day, but the great day never came. Thanks to somebody's foresight "up top" we never went to France but moved south instead to relieve a squadron down there, and incidentally to take part in the Dunkirk evacuation. Although events were moving rapidly, King Leopold had not yet given in and I don't think any of us fully realised what was so soon to happen around that onetime peaceful gateway to the Continent.

It was at five o'clock in the evening of May 25th that the squadron took off and headed south into the gathering dusk. Nature herself might have been warning us with that grey sky that all was not well and that a stern task lay ahead of us.

As we circled our new station and glided down towards the ground past the innumerable balloons of London's barrage, each standing out blackly against the sombre grey of the sky, it was already getting dark. The sections landed and taxied in to their dispersal points and their pilots climbed out. As they stood silently about waiting for the others to come in, a curl of smoke rose here and there from a cigarette. Apart from the cracking noise of the cooling exhausts, and an occasional remark in quiet tones, the only sound was the distant drone of a tractor bringing the tanker out to refuel the silent aircraft. It was very peaceful that evening of early summer, though so few miles away on the other side of the Channel hell was going on.

Having seen the aircraft refueled and ready for the morrow, we walked up to the mess, the sergeants giving us a quiet "Good night" as they left us to go to their own quarters. As we got nearer to the mess we could hear rounds of laughter and talking floating out across the lawns to disturb the silence. As we went in, our eyes blinking a protest against the sudden light, all was noise. Snatches of conversation hit our ears. "I gave him a squirt and he broke up and went straight in—," "Bill should be back soon. I saw him put it down on the beach and get out, so he's OK—" "…went into the drink. A destroyer picked me up—lucky for me it was going the right way," this from a pilot disguised as a seaman in a blue sweater, trousers and monkey jacket, which the Navy had given him when he was rescued.

I wandered, off to the bar to get a drink. A rather disheveled officer stood there with a glass in his hand talking to the barman. He turned as I came in. "Good Lord!"—"Well, I'm damned!" It was Ian (identity not known), who had been at F.T.S. with me. I hadn't seen him for years. He had left the Air Force and gone back to America some time back, but here he was again, once more in uniform.

We had a lot to talk about and I found that he had just returned from France. He had been shot down out there but had managed to get back to his aerodrome—only to find that his squadron had left for England. After sundry adventures he managed to elude the Germans, get to the coast and find a boat to bring him over. But except for the clothes he stood up in and a French tin hat he had taken from a poilu who would never need it again, he had lost everything he possessed. He was very proud of the tin hat. "Rather distinctive, what!" he said.

After supper the C.O., S/L Geoffrey Stephenson, called us together in the writing room, and introduced the C.O. of one of the other squadrons on the station who gave us some tips on the sort of thing we might now expect to get. It was while we were thus engaged that an orderly interrupted the talk by calling S/L James 'Prof' Leathart to the phone. When he came back he told us, "They wanted an aircraft to go over to Dunkirk and drop an important message. But the weather's too thick, never have found it in the dark; I told them so."

The long shadow of Dunkirk had fallen across our path, and to-morrow would come the reality. It was now getting late, so we gradually drifted off to bed. We had to be up in the morning in time to take off on patrol at seven o'clock. I don't know about the others, but I slept like a log.

Chapter 3

Dunkirk – First Patrol:
Morning, 26 May 1940

Save for a layer of hazy cloud high up in the sky, through which the sun shone mistily, the next morning dawned bright and clear. We ate our breakfasts in silence, and not much of it at that. Eggs and bacon don't sit too well on an excited stomach.

Smoking, talking, fourteen pilots assembled on the tarmac wondering who would be the unlucky two who would have to stay behind. We had brought twelve aircraft with us, and two extra pilots had come down by road the previous night. The section leaders alone looked quite happy, for they knew they were definite starters. For fairness we drew names out of a hat and face after face lighted up as its owner's name was called. In my flight the unlucky one was F/Sgt Unwin, and he stood looking at me with a hurt expression on his face, for all the world like a dog who has been told he can't come for a walk. I went over to try and console him, but he just shook his head sadly and said, "Well I'm damned, sir!"

I couldn't help it, I burst out laughing, while the other pilots shot humorous remarks at him.

"Go on, Grumpy, you'll live to fight another day!"... "Don't get too drunk while we're away!"

And that was why; from that time on, one flight-sergeant was called Grumpy.

We, the lucky ones, got into our aircraft and started up, the fitters fussing round the cockpits polishing mirrors and windscreens which were already spotless. A pat on the shoulder—"Good luck, sir. See 'em off good and proper!"—and they jumped down to guide their pilots out onto the aerodrome.

As we turned into wind and opened up, I noticed a lonely figure walking slowly back along the tarmac—it was Grumpy!

The C.O. was leading the squadron with a section of 'A' Flight, myself with a section on his right Wilf with one of "B Flight on his left and F/O Eric Ball (also referred to elsewhere as 'B') with a section, above and behind us all, the rearguard and lookout section.

We set course for Calais and climbed away south towards the thickening clouds over the French coast. Our instructions were to patrol Calais-Dunkirk at 17,000 feet. As we went higher and higher we kept running into straggling wisps of cloud, thin misty stuff which shone dazzlingly white in the light of the sun above. Below, the earth showed through as a dark mass, the Channel a slate grey ribbon with the reflected sun showing like a streak of silver paint down its middle.

We crossed the English coast at Dover. Ahead rose up a great black pall of smoke from Calais, drifting out in a long trail across the water. To the left another inky column showed the position of Dunkirk. There was something infinitely sad and terrible about that towering mass of smoke. I cannot describe just how I felt as I gazed fascinated on the dreadful scene, but I know that a surge of hatred for the Hun and all his filthy doings swept over me, and I felt that no mercy must be shown to a people who are a disgrace to humanity.

As these thoughts were racing through my mind, the C.O. turned and we flew up the coast towards Dunkirk. We were at 18,000 feet, just below the layer of high cloud; and turning at the other end of the patrol line we gradually lost height towards Calais. Suddenly from behind a bank of cloud, appeared twenty-one Ju 87 dive bombers, heading out to sea over Calais and looking like some sort of strange bird, with their big spotted undercarriages and upswept wings. We turned in behind them and closed to the attack.

The Huns flew on unheeding, apparently suffering from the delusion that we were their own fighter escort, until the leading section of Spitfires opened fire. Panic then swept the enemy formation. They split up in all directions, hotly pursued by nine Spitfires, while Eric & Co. kept watch behind us. I picked out one dive bomber and got on his tail, staying there as he twisted and turned this way and that, trying to avoid the eight streaks of tracer from my guns. Finally he pulled up and stalled, rolled over, and then plunged headlong towards the sea out of control.

I felt happy! I had often wondered what it would be like really to shoot at an aircraft and bring it down. Now I knew, and it was definitely exhilarating! I turned to try and take stock of how the fight was progressing. Two other Stukas were spinning down, and several Spitfires were wheeling about over Calais looking for more targets. I soon found one for myself, a Stuka just starting his dive on to the town. I plunged after him firing at long range in the hope of putting him off. I saw him release his bomb, and then he was away as fast as he could go, heading east over the trees. I had turned and climbed up over the town again when Eric's voice came over the R/T: "Fighters, fighters!" A pause, then, "My God, there are hundreds of them!" This was an exaggeration, but there were about fifty, and I couldn't help smiling at his tone of voice.

There weren't many Stukas left now, but Eric turned and tried to hold off the German fighters, Me 109s, while we completed the rout. But before we could complete this job the 109s were down on us. A burst of tracer came over my left wing and I turned violently as a grey painted shape with black crosses on it flashed past. I saw the pink blur of the pilot's face turned towards me as he passed, and then another darker shape, only yards in front of my airscrew, flashed after him. It was a Spitfire after that 109.

To my left I saw P/O P.V. Watson, hot on the tail of a Hun. As I watched, I saw another Me 109 get on Watty's tail. I switched on my transmitter and yelled a warning to him, at the same time turning to try and cut the second Hun off. Even as I did so I saw a flash on the Spitfire as a cannon shell hit it. The Spitfire went into a steep dive, smoke pouring from the engine. I circled and saw a white puff as a parachute blossomed out far below.

The noise of machine-gun fire behind me suddenly reminded me that I was still in the game, and I found that three Messerschmitts were honouring me with their undivided attention. An awful fear gripped the pit of my stomach. I knew I had very little ammunition left, probably only enough for one burst, and three to one wasn't so funny. I pulled round in a tight turn, the aircraft shuddering just above the stall. I knew I could outturn the 109's but I had very little petrol to play with now as well as being short of ammunition, and obviously it was time to go home!

The leading 109 was firing short burst every now and then, his tracer going behind me as he strove to get his sights far enough ahead of me. I remember I was cursing at the top of my voice. I was in a jam, I was frightened, and I was furious with those Huns for making me frightened. Something had to be done and done quickly. I tightened the turn still more. The aircraft flicked as she stalled. I rolled over on my back and out into a reverse turn, a trick I had learnt back at F.T.S. This manoeuvre temporarily got me away from the Huns and I dived hell for leather towards the sea, flattening out as near the water as I could and then opening the throttle wide.

I was beginning to breathe again when rat-tat-tat behind me and a tracer appeared over the cockpit, the bullets churning up a patch of foam in the water a hundred yards ahead. It was then that I remembered the automatic boost cut-out, a device giving maximum power from the engine for use in an emergency. I pushed the lever down and felt the surge of power from the Merlin in front of me as the aircraft accelerated. Twisting and turning, I managed to keep clear of the Hun bullets, very nearly hitting the water several times while doing so. One of the 109's had evidently climbed up to one side and now came diving at me from the beam. I turned towards him and gave him the last of my ammunition at point-blank range. I think he went straight in, for as I drew well away with my superior speed I could see only two Messerschmitts behind me.

At last I saw the white cliffs of Dover, never a more welcome sight than now, and feeling sick and rather limp I throttled back, climbed up to clear the cliffs and flew on to the aerodrome.

As I circled, putting everything out before coming in to land, I noticed three other Spitfires already on the ground refuelling. I had barely touched down when another appeared from the south, roared low over the aerodrome and came in. My crew came running out to meet me as I taxied in, caught the wing-tips and guided me to the tanker.

With a sigh of relief I switched off and climbed stiffly out of the cockpit whilst and army of armourers fell on the aircraft and reloaded the guns at top speed. A crowd of airmen and pilots surrounded me, questions were shot at me right and left. Before I could collect my wits and answer, the Intelligence Officer pushed his way through, handed me the green Combat Report form, and guided me to the tailplane. "Come on! The report first please. You can talk to the chaps afterwards." Slowly I tried to sort out all the thoughts racing through my head and remember the sequence of events.

"How many did you get, first? I want the final score."

"I got a Ju 87 and I'm pretty certain I got a 109 as well."

"Good show," he said, and made a note in his little book.

At last I had finished writing out my report and more pilots had returned. After a while no more came in and ten pilots trooped back to the mess, smoking and talking for all they were worth.

"I saw one of our kites spinning down. Nobody stepped out."

"I saw Watty go down, but he got out." Eventually we decided it was the C.O. we had seen spinning. Sgt Jack Potter had seen that the pilot who baled out was wearing black overalls. Watty had been in black overalls, the C.O. in white. Rather sadly we reached the mess, to flop down somewhat exhausted in an armchair, have a well-earned drink and count the score. Seven Ju 87's and three 109's certain, and one Me 109 probably destroyed. Not bad for the first show.

Our casualties were the C.O. and Watty missing, and Eric unserviceable with a crease across his forehead made by a bullet from one of those Me 109's and a flesh wound in his arm.

"I thought I was dead," he said amidst roars of laughter. "Then I saw some more tracer coming past me, so I came to the conclusion I must still be alive."

A very near thing, but with an Me 109 to his credit he was more than quits.

Chapter 4

More Patrols:
Afternoon, 26 May 1940-27 May 1940

In the meantime the N.C.O.s and crews were working like niggers, patching bullet-holes and checking everything over, to get the aircraft serviceable for the next patrol. I had only two bullet-holes in the wings of my kite, and two strikes on the tail, where bullets had been deflected. Those Huns must have been darned bad shots! But some of the other aircraft were worse off than mine, one of the other sections having seventeen holes in the fuselage.

By lunch-time we had mustered seven aircraft, and soon after we managed to get nine serviceable. A quick lunch and we were down on the tarmac again. As acting C.O. I was leading the squadron this time, and nine Spitfires taxied out and took off, the thundering roar of the Merlins reverberating across the 'drome.

We circled and climbed away south-east, the sun shining and glinting on our wings. It was a lovely afternoon. Several broken layers of cloud hung across the sky, the lowest being at about 9,000 feet. As we neared the French coast, I decided to patrol below this bottom layer, as it was obvious that any bombers knocking about would be flying below it in order to see their target; and at the same time it afforded us protection against a surprise attack from above.

We flew up and down that stretch of coast which was to become so familiar to us. Half an hour passed, and still nothing happened, though we scanned the ground below eagerly for bomb bursts and the sky above for enemy aircraft. Suddenly came a shout from the lookout man: "Eight 109's right above!"

We had come out into a clear patch just north of Calais and the Huns had evidently emerged from the clouds now behind us. I looked round but could see nothing.

"Where are they? I can't see them!"

"Right above us. About a thousand feet. Look out, they've seen us, they're coming down!"

I pulled round in a steep turn to the right, the rest of the squadron spreading out in line astern behind me. By this time we were over a convenient patch of cloud, and as I circled I saw a Spitfire dive into the cloud with a 109 on its tail. It was F/O Gordon Sinclair, who was leading his section. I turned to follow, but the Hun pulled up clear of the clouds and climbed away inland. I opened the throttle wide and climbed after him, keeping a good look-out behind in case anything was after me. The sky was clear of aircraft. Half a minute before there had been seventeen aircraft within that small clear patch. Now, in the miraculous manner which defeats the logic of the eye, there was only that Hun and myself.

I was overtaking fast, just below and behind him. He obviously had no idea I was there. Carefully I maneuvered my sights on to him and then slightly ahead, to get the deflection. Then I let him have it. It must have given him the shock of his life if he knew anything about it at all. His aircraft lurched, fell over almost on its back and went screaming vertically down. I half rolled and followed him, in case he was shamming, although I knew I had got him with that one carefully aimed burst. Down, down I went, watching for him to pull out, but he never did. I suddenly realised that I was perilously low myself, and doing a fair rate of knots as well. I had lost sight of my Hun, and realised he must have hit the ground by now; for he had been well below me and still in a vertical dive.

I pulled back on the stick and felt my head droop forward. At the same time everything went purple and then black in front of my eyes as I "blacked out." I came round again, climbed out to sea and made once more towards the clouds. Looking at my watch I noticed that only about three minutes had elapsed since the beginning of the fight. It had felt like a quarter of an hour at least.

I wondered how the rest of the chaps had got on. The English coast slipped by underneath me. Ahead the tower of Canterbury Cathedral shone in the sun and the Estuary glinted beyond. I came to Manston aerodrome, circling to see if anybody had landed there to refuel. Yes there was a Spitfire just landing. I dived and flew low across the aerodrome, noting the letters on the fuselage as I flashed by. It was one of ours. A glance at my petrol gauge showed that my fuel was getting low, so I came in and taxied up to where the other Spitfire was parked. As I switched off, Gordon walked over to me. He was swearing like a trooper.

"What's the matter with you?" I demanded.

"Did you see that little swine on my tail? Well, he got young Ball. I saw him spinning."

"Blast him," I said. "Well, I got him, anyway, so we're quits. He climbed up after you went into that cloud, and I tailed him. He never knew what hit him and went straight in. Did you get anything yourself?"

"Yes, I got one of them after I came out of the cloud. A flamer."

"Good show. That's two, anyway."

Another Spitfire came in and taxied towards us. Out stepped young Ball. We looked at him as though he were a ghost.

"Didn't you go into a spin when that Hun had a crack at you?" asked Gordon.

"Oh, yes, but I came out and everybody had disappeared, so I came back."

Gordon and I looked at each other. "I wish you wouldn't give people such frights," said Gordon, "I thought he'd got you."

One by one more Spitfires came in. I got on the phone to

our own station to see if anybody had turned up there. None had, which meant two were missing, P/O Michael Lyne and Sgt C.A. Irwin.

But after the aircraft had been refueled and we had been up to the mess for a cup of tea, we flew back to our own station and found that news had come through that Michael had parked down on the beach at Deal with a bullet in his knee. Sgt Irwin was still missing, though.

The following day was dull, with huge banks of grey cumulus cloud cutting off the sun. But in the afternoon it cleared, and the evening turned to perfect summer weather, without a cloud in the sky, as we took off after tea. The Operations Room had rung through to tell us that there would be "hell over Dunkirk this evening" and it was with a tremendous feeling of excitement that we climbed up over the aerodrome and settled down on the now familiar course over the Thames for Dunkirk. Once past the Estuary we could already see, miles away, the huge black column of smoke from the burning oil-tanks, rearing up nightmare fashion into the quiet evening sky.

Soon we were out over the sea and in a few minutes came to Dunkirk, turning eastward to run up the coast to Nieuport past those rolling yellow sand-dunes and beaches on which a chapter of Britain's history was beginning to be enacted.

The sea far below shone blue and gold under the westering sun. Above us was the deep blue dome of the heavens. Anxiously we scanned it, looking for the tell-tale glint of the sun on a pair of wings which would show us the enemy was above. Suddenly, just off the south mole of Dunkirk harbour below, appeared three white circles in the water near a tanker which was lying off-shore. Bombs! Frantically I searched the sky to the right of us, trying to see the aircraft which had dropped them. It was the barrage put up by our anti-aircraft batteries which showed me his position. There was only one enemy aircraft.

Thinking it might be a decoy, I called up Wilf on the R/T and told him to stay on patrol while I took a section after the Hun. I turned away to give chase, but I think the Hun must have seen us, for he immediately turned inland, pursued by bursts of Ack-Ack. We crossed the coast diving slightly, as our quarry was below us. Gradually we overtook him, to find the enemy aircraft was a Henschel Hs 126. As we neared him he began to turn and twist this way and that, the sun catching the dark green camouflage and the black crosses on his wings. I came up with him rather fast over Ypres and gave him a short burst as he turned back underneath me. Although he had a far slower aircraft he used his maneuverability to escape our fire and fought us off magnificently, and after another burst I lost him as he dived away behind me. Feeling that we shouldn't really be playing with a Henschel miles inside Belgium when we were supposed to be guarding the Dunkirk beaches, I called up the section to rejoin formation. F/O Frankie Brinsden, my No.2, was soon beside me making faces, as apparently he had found the Hun again, but Grumpy was not to be seen. The two of us dived down and tore back at twenty feet over the peaceful Belgium countryside. I tried to spot signs of either Germans or our own troops, but not a soul could be seen. Cattle browsing in the fields seemed to be the only living things in a deserted landscape. We passed over farms and villages all equally deserted, and then the dunes of the coast showed in front of us. As we flashed over the beaches and out to sea I saw hundreds of khaki-clad figures on the front and among the dunes waving to us as we went by. Under the huge black pall of smoke that hung over the town and drifted slowly out to sea it was almost like full night.

Out of reach of any German guns we climbed up again trying to find the rest of the squadron. I called Grumpy and heard him answer faintly. He was telling me his position, but I could not quite get what he said, though I did' hear his triumphant voice repeating, "I got him, I got him!"

Later on I had his story. When that Henschel had seen

Frankie and me reform and turn back, he had thought himself safe, whereupon Grumpy, sitting unsuspected above him in the sun, had dived on him and sent him crashing into a field with his engine on fire.

But to go back a little, we still continued our patrol, having fetched up with two aircraft of "B" Flight, but at last I called up the others and said we were going home, and we turned north-west towards our supper. As we came to the aerodrome in the dusk and sank down to Mother Earth the balloons of London seemed to be made of gold and silver. The weather was still beautiful and calm.

Soon after the rest of the squadron arrived. They had been lucky. Wilf, searching the sky for a target and wondering where I had got to, suddenly espied a Dornier just ahead and above him. He attacked and the Dornier burst into flames, plunging like a comet down into the blue water below. A few minutes later he saw two more, and a section between them sent down one of these on his last long dive to the sea. The ear-splitting "blue note" of his over-revving engines must have sounded like music to the weary troops on the sands, ending abruptly as he hit the water far below in a huge cascade of white foam.

The other Dornier, the third, had suffered a similar fate at the hands of Sgt Bernard Jennings, and then, petrol getting low and no more Huns being in sight, they had followed us back.

I pounced on Grumpy after we landed. "Why didn't you join up when I told you to?" I demanded. "I must have had my R/T switched off, sir!" he said with a sly grin.

"You're a damned liar," I said, unable to suppress a smile. "You know perfectly well you heard me call up." His grin just got a bit wider. I added: "It was a good show, your getting him like that, but you obey orders in future."

He was still grinning as we said "Good night," before parting to go up to our respective messes.

Chapter 5

First Wing Patrol:
28 May 1940-30 May 1940

Up to now we had encountered two big snags. In the first place we were operating at the limit of our operational range—we could only stay on patrol for a maximum time of one hour—and secondly we were almost always outnumbered.

The latter disadvantage was temporarily overcome on the following day, May 28th, when the three Spitfire squadrons on the station took off together and patrolled as a wing. The Huns were now beginning to escort their bombers more strongly, and the idea was that the leading squadron of the wing should take on the bombers whilst the other two tackled the fighter escort.

This was the first time we had tried operating as a wing, and on this first patrol we met with quite a fair measure of success. The weather was dull, with big masses of thundery-looking cloud covering the sky, the base varying from 5,000 to about 10,000 feet. We hadn't been on patrol long when the leading squadron dived away through a fantastic ravine in the mountainous black clouds and disappeared from view. Although we gave chase we weren't able to find them again, but we found something else instead.

As we emerged from the valley between the towering clouds into an open space I suddenly spied, just above and in front of us, about sixty Me 109's and a dozen Spitfires in a tremendous dogfight. Climbing as fast as I could, and keeping clear of the fight, I circled round the edge of this cloud arena until I had reached the height of the combatants. The squadron behind me then broke up and dived into the fight. As I went in I saw five more 109's come diving out of a tunnel high up in the black wall of cloud on my right, and then another five, and another. By this time I was well into the battle, and as a Hun crossed my nose I turned after him and closed in on his tail. Glancing in my mirror I saw coming round in a turn behind me another 109. "I'll have to be quick getting the one in front," I thought, "before his pal gets on my tail."

I got my sights on and pressed the firing button. My guns fired, but only very slowly and spasmodically. I swore as another glance in the mirror showed me Hun No. 2 just on my tail. Then I half rolled and let the aircraft plummet down in the ensuing dive until the clock showed 400 m.p.h. Slowly, I eased back on the stick, feeling my eyelids and head grow heavy with the pressure that was pressing me down in my seat. But now I was out of the dive and soaring up and up, the black wall of cloud in front of me dropping out of sight below the nose of the aircraft as it reached the vertical. I tilted my head back to watch the clouds on the opposite side come slowly down to meet the nose as the aircraft came over on its back at the top of the loop. Then I eased the stick forward and to the right and rolled out right way up.

This had brought me out to one side of the dogfight, and at the same height, and I cruised around, trying to find the cause of the gun trouble. I looked at my air-gauge, which showed the pressure in the compressed air-bottle operating the guns, and it read 80 lbs. I swore again. No wonder the guns wouldn't fire properly. I wondered if I had been hit; a bullet might have struck a pipeline, causing a leak.

However, I turned into the fight again to have another squirt and see what happened. A 109 saw me coming and turned to meet me. Tracer appeared from his guns and passed just underneath my starboard wing. Not a bad shot, as I was a rather awkward target from his position. I turned hard to the left as we passed and slowly began to come round on his tail.

He suddenly came out of his turn and gave me a fleeting shot, but as I pressed the button there, was a single "crack" and a single bullet sped on its way.

"That's a fat lot of good," I thought, seeing the Hun rolling away out of sight below me. I pressed the button again but nothing happened at all. There didn't seem much point in sticking around in the middle of so many Huns with guns that didn't work, so I dived down into the clouds and flattened out below them at 2,000 feet. Looking at my watch I saw that only five minutes had elapsed since we first sighted the Huns!

Suddenly coming towards me I saw three twin-engined aircraft. If these were Heinkels I was going to look an awful twirp. But as I got nearer I saw they were Ansons and heaved a sigh of relief. The worthy Coastal Command pilots, however, apparently did not recognise me so easily, for they turned in line astern into a tight circle. I rocked my wings and circled round them. They still appeared suspicious, but eventually straightened up and continued on their way whilst I steered for home.

As I climbed out of the cockpit my crew came up. "Did you get anything, sir?"

"Not a ruddy thing," I said in disgust. "There's no air in the bottle, it must be leaking." I added, "I only fired about twenty rounds before the guns petered out." Grimacing their disappointment the men started in to check the air system.

I was one of the first down but one by one the others came in until all had returned! Good show, no one missing! I wandered round talking to the others as they climbed out. F/Sgt Steere and Grumpy claimed one each, both flamers. Several of the others thought they had got one but they couldn't claim as they did not see what had happened to their opponent. As Wilf put it, "There wasn't time to see anything. I just fired when something came into my sights and then turned like hell as something fired at me! What a party!"

It seemed amazing that everybody had come back from that fight. I had a word with Grumpy and Steere. Grumpy was grinning happily, but Steere only made a face.

"What's the matter?" I said.

"I got one in flames and the poor swine got stuck half-way out of the cockpit. Rotten sight." And he turned away to light a cigarette.

Back in the mess we learned how the other squadrons had fared. Two pilots were missing but the next day one of them returned. He had parked down on the beach at Dunkirk and had got back on a destroyer. He reported that he had seen two 109's come down in flames and two more go straight into the sea. The leading squadron had sighted some Dorniers and given chase, when we had lost them in the clouds.

That evening the weather cleared and after dinner I was strolling in the garden in front of the mess when Wilf, standing on the lawn, called me over. "What does that remind you of?" he asked, pointing above his head. I looked up and saw a cloud of gnats milling about in the evening air, looking for all the world like that dogfight in the morning.

We both laughed.

Next day the two other squadrons went to another station and were relieved by two more squadrons, both of which had at one time or another been on the same station with us. They both had grand C.O.s in S/L H.W. 'Tubby' Mermagen (222 Sqn) and S/L Robin Hood (41 Sqn). We were now the veteran squadron on the station, and after one or two wing patrols during the course of which nothing was seen, it was decided that we should lead the wing to try and change the luck. For two fruitless days it seemed as though we were still going to be unlucky, but on June 1st things really happened.

Chapter 6

Dawn Patrol:
Dawn, 1 June 1940

On June 1st the wing was on the dawn patrol. Still full of sleep we rolled out of bed at 3. 15 a.m. and staggered downstairs to the anteroom for tea and biscuits. Then down to the tarmac, to the rising and falling thunder of noise as fitters ran up the engines, to the sight of dim aircraft, shown up by the blue flames from the exhausts which stabbed the half light.

Still dazed with sleep I climbed into the cockpit, tested the oxygen supply and the R/T and then taxied out to the far end of the aerodrome and turned into wind, there to sit yawning whilst the other aircraft formed up around me. Thumbs up from each section leader and I waved my hand over my head, the signal to take off, and opened up.

A throbbing roar all around cut off the outside world as we sped across the aerodrome. The bumps from the undercart became less and less, until with a final bump we beat gravity and the green blur of grass slipped away beneath us. My right hand dropped to the undercart control, moved it back, and then felt for the pump. A few seconds later two faint thuds told me the wheels were up, and with a confirming glance at the cockpit indicator I reached behind me and pulled the hood shut. Changing hands on the stick, I closed the radiator and put the airscrew into coarse pitch, throttling back to cruising revs., and then glanced at the rev. counter, boost and oil-gauges to make sure that everything was O.K.

As I turned left round the drome I glanced in the mirror to see the rest of the squadron formed up behind me. Three circuits and the other two squadrons were in position, S/L

Mermagen, 'Tubby' to everybody, immediately behind us and Robin (S/L Hood) bringing up the rear with his squadron.

I straightened up and climbed away towards Dunkirk and the rising sun, circling as we left the English coast to pick up a fourth squadron of Spitfires from another aerodrome which had a rendezvous with us. Then out over the North Sea, forty-eight Spitfires looking for trouble!

When we reached the Belgian coast I turned left run up to Nieuport, past the packed beaches looking oddly like Blackpool or Margate on a Bank Holiday, past the hundreds of small craft lying offshore to ferry those heroic troops to the bigger vessels standing farther out. Every kind of craft was represented there, Thames barges, lighters, rowing boats, lifeboats, in fact anything that would float. Stretching back towards the cliffs of England was an unending stream of ships, some taking precious loads from the hell beneath us now to the comparative peace and safety of our island, others returning in the opposite direction, back to the inferno to save some more of that undefeatable little army.

From 5,000 feet we watched the drama being enacted below us. Above was a thin layer of cloud, not more than fifty feet thick, through which the sun was just visible. Suddenly in front of us appeared a twin-engined aircraft followed by eleven more, all heading towards Nieuport. I switched on the R/T: "Twelve Me 110's straight ahead, I said, then opened the throttle and gave chase.

The Messerschmitts evidently saw us coming, for they went into a circle and tried to get into the clouds. For once the odds were in our favour, and four to one at that. I was still out of firing range when, to my astonishment, one of the enemy aircraft staggered and then plummeted down, down with a strange pendulum motion as its tail came off. None of my section had fired, and since we were leading and out of range still, I could not imagine how on earth the Hun had been shot down.

By now we had closed with the enemy and turning right I got on the tail of a Messerschmitt and chased him down as he dived away, the rest of the squadrons fighting to get a target! It really was pathetic. By our standards of training those pilots should never have left F.T.S., yet here they were; trying to fight four times their number and with no idea of how to do it. War is war but I remember cursing the Hun for a cold-blooded devil in sending out pilots like these to fight us. Even as I cursed I realised what a queer thought this was. We ought to he thankful for cold meat like this!

I fired several bursts at the 110 I was after and saw his port motor splutter and stop. As he tried to turn away I pulled round inside him and gave him another squirt, this time hitting his starboard engine, which was immediately enveloped in smoke. By this time we were pretty low, and as I pulled up I saw him go down into the deck.

Looking round I was in time to see the tail come off another 110, and down he went too.

Since every Hun in sight had a Spitfire on his tail I climbed up through the clouds to see if there were anything left up there. As I came out on top I saw two Spitfires cruising about. As any Me 110's came up through the cloud they jumped on them, sending them down again. Unfortunately for those wretched Huns the cloud was too thin to hide in—there was no escape. I came down again, and as a Me 110 came towards me head on, I fired, then turned to come back after him. But another Spitfire was on his tail before I could get there. A few seconds later a dull flash appeared on the ground below, followed by a huge tongue of flame. And that was another Nazi less in the world.

After this there didn't seem to be any more Huns left, so I dived down almost to the water and came home, there to find most of the aircraft already on the ground. Two more came in as I was landing, and the squadron was complete.

The second squadron came in by ones and twos, and then the third squadron in formation. The latter had apparently not seen much and had been unable to find anything to fire at.

The first pilot I saw as I climbed out of my aircraft was Sgt Jennings. He was grinning from ear to ear. "How many did you get, sir?" he called.

"One," I answered.

"Only one, sir! I got two"

I grinned myself "If people like you weren't so damned greedy, I might be able to get a few more!"

A car pulled up by the aircraft and F/O J.H.E. 'Cras' Crastor, our intelligence officer, stepped out.

"Good morning, gentlemen. Any luck?"

A chorus answered him, whereupon he was heard to mutter a few remarks about the unearthly hour at which he was forced to rise, merely on account of bloodthirsty young devils whose idea of fun was a fight before breakfast.

Having received our reports Crastor counted up the score. Seven 110's had been accounted for, and three 109's.

I hadn't seen any 109's and said so, whereupon it turned out that Wilf, with "B" Flight, had had a little private dogfight with some 109's which had appeared out of nowhere. "B" Flight had apparently made the best of it! As for the 110's, Sgt Jennings had got two, and so had Sinclair, and Grumpy, Ball and I had each got one.

Back in the mess it was still too early for breakfast, so, we sat about in the anteroom swapping yarns. Tubby Mermagen, who had been responsible for shooting down the first 110, told us a really *stirring* tale. Literally, I mean, for Tubby volunteered the information that the miracle had been achieved by use of his *stirring* attack. By stirring it was discovered he meant stirring the stick round the cockpit once his sights were on, thereby getting a hosepipe effect from his guns. This, then, was the secret of how to shoot down a Hun when at 1,200 yards range! However, another of his pilots had got an Me 110 by means of more orthodox methods. Two more pilots were missing, apparently shot down by Flak.

But any patrol that Tubby was on invariably turned out to be an amusing one, at any rate in retrospect when he got back to the mess. He was a great humorist, and now he improved the shining hour until breakfast by giving an exhibition of his actions and reactions on a previous patrol when he had found himself short of oxygen. He had us all rocking in our seats with laughter. It was the first time I ever remember being convulsed with mirth at such an hour of the morning!

Chapter 7

Dunkirk – the Last Patrols:
Morning, 1 June 1940-4 June 1940

Breakfast over, we went down, again on to the tarmac. The order of battle was as before. Again we circled as we left the coast to pick up the other squadron, then out over the glassy sea, down the long line of ships to Dunkirk.

The weather had not changed since dawn, and as the enemy bombers would have to come below the thin layer of cloud in order to drop their eggs, I decided to patrol just below the cloud base again.

As I turned off the harbour I glanced back over my shoulder at the mass of aircraft stretching away behind. It was an impressive sight, and I only hope it cheered up those poor devils five thousand feet below us on the shore.

Nieuport slowly appeared beneath my wings, and I turned to run back down the coast. I had just turned again at Dunkirk, and was heading back once more, when something moving on my left caught my eye. I looked round in time to see an aircraft diving down towards the shipping off the harbour. Coming hard round I dived after it, the rest of the squadron chasing after me. The aircraft flattened out over a destroyer for a moment and then turned, climbing towards the coast. As I followed there was a terrific flash below and a huge fountain of water was flung high into the air, to fall slowly back into the sea. As the disturbance subsided I saw that the destroyer had completely disappeared. So the aircraft in front of me was a Hun. A blind fury gripped me.

I was gaining on him as he strove to reach the safety of the clouds, but he was into them before I could get close enough to fire. I went up through the clouds in the hope of finding him, but he had disappeared. As I circled, waiting to see if he would appear again, some anti-aircraft fire inland attracted my attention and I caught sight of three Dorniers just above the clouds. Easing the stick forward I dropped down until I was almost in the clouds and then began to stalk the quarry. I don't think they saw me until I came round behind them and came up into position to attack. The Huns were flying in "Vic" formation and I picked out toe right-hand aircraft, closing in behind him. I fired a short burst from about 400 yards in the hope of killing the rear gunner, or at any rate frightening him.

As I closed in to shorter range, another Spitfire climbed out of the clouds to the left and turned in behind the left-hand Dornier. I grinned to myself, then concentrated on holding my aircraft steady in the slipstream from the Hun in front of me as the sights came on to his fuselage. My right thumb felt for the firing button on the stick and pressed it. A muffled "B-r-r-r-p" came from the wings and I felt the aircraft check slightly as eight streams of tracer spanned the space between us.

The Spitfire bumped in the slipstream and my sights drifted off the target. I stopped firing to correct the aim and noticed tracer from the Dornier passing over my left wing. Then— "Spang!" and I looked down to see a shining furrow along the top of the wing, where a bullet had bounced off the metal taking a sliver of paint with it.

I fired again, and as the Hun seemed to rush back to meet me broke away down to one side, muscles tense as involuntarily I tried to contract my body, half expecting to hear the sound of bullets hitting the aircraft. I made a good target for the German gunner before I got safely out of range. If he fired he missed me, and as I flattened out I saw the Dornier losing height very unsteadily and disappearing into the cloud. I dived down and searched frantically for him, as one more burst seemed to be all that was needed to put paid to his account. But I couldn't see a Dornier anywhere, so I made a few remarks about the parentage of the pilot and of Huns in general and turned out towards the sea.

Crossing the coast again a Heinkel passed just in front of me and I tagged on behind and gave him a couple of squirts as he climbed into the cloud. By this time my windscreen had become covered in oil, owing as I later found out to a leak in the airscrew, and it was impossible to see through the glass or use the sight. I was getting more and more annoyed, and when two more Heinkels in tight formation appeared above me I had to open the hood, pull down my goggles and peer round the edge of the windscreen in order to see what I was firing at.

A terrific blast of air hit my head as I, looked out, nearly knocking my goggles off. Closing in below and to one side of the Huns I gave them the last of my ammunition, though without much hope of hitting them. But at least it had the effect of sending them up into the cloud, and as they melted like ghosts into the grey vapour above I turned and dived down to the water and headed out along the line of ships for England.

As we had run into the first lot of Huns only when it was almost time to go home, I was by now getting very short of petrol. Ten feet above the sea I raced along past the strange collection of vessels heading from hell to heaven. A mile ahead I recognised a cross-Channel steamer. I smiled to myself, remembering the long hours I had spent on her in happier days, crossing, to the Continent. She would take a good two hours more to get home now, whereas I would be there in ten minutes.

Just as I came abreast of the ship the whole sea suddenly erupted immediately behind her, and only a few hundred yards away from me. I nearly jumped out of the cockpit, with fright!

I had been rudely awakened from my dreaming by a Dornier sitting at about 2,000 feet, nearly over the top of me. As I looked, four little black objects left the belly of the bomber and came hurtling down towards the ship. I turned sharply and began to climb as hard as I could, feeling absolutely wild that the Hun had given me such a fright. He looked so insolent, sitting up there throttled right back and letting his eggs go in that deliberate fashion. Luckily for me it hadn't helped him to aim accurately, but I felt like ramming him. I was not, however, forced to dwell further on this suicidal measure, for the Hun then turned back towards the French coast and climbed away as hard as he could, pursued by bursts of A.-A. fire from a cruiser a mile or so to the north-east. Looking at the cruiser I watched the flickering stabs of flame from one of her "Chicago Pianos." Though it certainly looked a wicked and deadly performance enough, I couldn't see whether the Dornier was hit or not.

Once more I turned for home, on again up the line of ships, over the rusty wrecks on the Goodwin Sands, glistening like gold in the sun, and then the coast slipped by beneath me. I landed at Manston to refuel, then back over the peaceful English countryside to our own aerodrome.

A myriad silver dots ahead, the balloons of London, told me I was nearly home, and soon the aerodrome hove in sight. Usually I was never able to find it easily and spent the last few miles looking everywhere for a glimpse of some hangers, finally, just as I was beginning to think I had passed it, finding it as a rule hidden from view beneath the nose or a wing. But to-day I hit it straight off for once. As I sighted the hangars I put the nose down and dived across the aerodrome, to pull up in a climbing turn to the left round the circuit, throttling back as I did so. My left hand went up to the hood catch, pulling the hood open far enough for me to put my elbow against it and push it right back.

The airspeed dropped to 180 m.p.h.; I pulled down the under carriage selector, and the little white indicator pegs in the wings came slowly out until I could read "Down" in red letters on both of them. A glance at the electric indicator in the cockpit told me that the wheels were locked down. Then I opened the radiator wide.

The speed had now dropped to 160 m.p.h., and throttling back still more as I turned at the downwind side of the aerodrome I waited until the clock showed 120 and then pulled down the lever to lower the flaps. I felt the aircraft slow up, the nose dropping slightly at the same time. I pulled the control to put the airscrew into fine pitch, then—stick over to the left a little and back, and the aircraft was gliding into wind towards the aerodrome. I pulled the throttle back and felt it stop. Then I remembered the mixture control was still forward in the "weak position" and was preventing the throttle from being closed. I pulled it back and then closed the throttle more as a belt of trees slid by underneath and the boundary fence came to meet me. A glance at the air-speed indicator—95 m.p.h., O.K.—and I closed the throttle completely, easing the stick back as I passed over the fence. Back a little more still as the aircraft flattened out—hold it!—then right back, and a second later some jolting and a slight bump from the tail. We were down.

Pulling the brake lever to and fro, I eased the brakes on and off to slow down without tipping up on the nose, and gradually came to a standstill. A glance behind as I put the flaps up showed me that nobody else was coming in, and I turned and taxied to the dispersal point and switched off. My fitter jumped up on the wing as I took my helmet off.

"Any luck, sir?"

I grimaced. "Look at that ruddy windscreen!"

The fitter frowned and shook his head. "Sorry, sir. It's the airscrew, I'm afraid. It's very bad on this kite."

I climbed out, lit a cigarette' and wandered over to where a group of pilots stood talking to Crastor and making out their combat reports. As I approached, Crastor turned and held out a green form.

But I shook my head. "No luck, I am afraid. I pushed a Dornier into the clouds looking a bit shaky, but I f couldn't find him again. He may have come down but I can't claim."

"Bad luck."

Everybody was talking and asking questions. Bit by bit I. began to get an idea of what had happened to the others. Sinclair had got two, a Heinkel and a Dornier, both on fire, F/O Leonard. A. 'Ace' Haines had got a "probable" (a Heinkel), and so had Grumpy and Sgt Jennings. Sgt Potter was missing.

"Not so good," somebody remarked. "That damned cloud was just ideal for them. It was a bit thicker than it was this morning."

Still talking we wended our way up to the mess, to sit at our ease for the rest of the morning, drinking on the lawn. Robin had the best tale to tell. He had led his squadron after some Ju 88s up towards Ostend, and on the way back, having finished his ammunition, he had met a Hun going home. They passed each other at a respectful distance.

A few minutes later the same thing happened again, by which time Robin was getting a bit annoyed. When, a few miles out to sea, he saw another one, he couldn't stand it any longer and charged straight at the Hun as if to ram him. They were both very low over the water, and to his absolute amazement the wretched Boche dived straight into the sea.

"Pity I hadn't got just one bullet left," he said. "I could have claimed it then."

Next day we did another patrol, but all was quiet over on the other side. The evacuation of Dunkirk appeared to be completed. When we landed at the aerodrome again we were overjoyed to find that Sgt Potter had got back. A bullet in his oil-tank had forced him to come down in the sea, and he had been picked up by a French fishing boat, the *Jolie Mascot*. Her captain was trying to get back to Dunkirk from England but had got himself lost. Potter took over the duties of navigator and got his craft to the Belgian coast, where he took part in the rescue operations, finally coming back with some of the last of the B.E.F. A darned fine show.

Another early patrol on June 3rd, and then the next day the last show we were to do before going back to our home station. At 4 a.m: we were taxi-ing out, and took off flight by flight. The clouds were at 200 feet and completely covered the sky, but we managed to rendezvous above them, and after circling for a while picked up the other two squadrons. We then set course to pick up the fourth squadron from Rochford, and more by luck than anything else met them just as they came through the cloud. Then the wing set off on the familiar course.

The wind was south-east and the smoke from Dunkirk stretched right to London, a black ninety-mile trail! Over on the other side there was no activity to be seen. A few derelict Thames barges, a sunken destroyer, an overturned lorry on the beach, such were the only reminders of the conflict now over. Only the pall of smoke, greater than ever now that our own demolition people had been around doing their particular job.

The whole scene rather reminded me of a theatre after the audience has gone. Nothing to remind one of the show but the litter left behind. Yes, the show was over now. The enemy was within twenty miles of our coasts, but another show would be put on, many shows perhaps, and Hitler would never speak the last line.

Chapter 8

Nocturne Militaire:
5 June 1940-30 June 1940

On June 5th we took off from the aerodrome for the last time and headed away towards our home station. It was with some regret that we left. We had had a grand time there and everybody, from the Station Commander downwards, had been kindness itself. Nothing had been too much trouble if it had helped us at all.

Our stay had been very successful too. We had succeeded in destroying 28 German aircraft and probably destroying nine others. This for the loss of the C.O. (prisoner of war), two pilots killed, 'Watty' and Sgt Irwin, and one wounded, Michael. Ball and John had been slightly wounded but were fit again. Not bad arithmetic at all.

It was Ball and John who were to be the next pilots in action, but more of that later. As we headed home our thoughts were dwelling on leave. W/C A.B. Woodhall, our Station Commander, had promised us forty-eight hours when we got back, and I think we all felt very carefree and happy as we came over the aerodrome, went into our own special formation, and one by one peeled off to come screaming across the aerodrome. One by one we landed and taxied up to our dispersal point, to be met by a smiling Woody and S/L Philip Pinkham, our new C.O. Then to the Mess for some drinks before lunch, with everybody shooting questions at us. We managed to answer most of them, I think, and cleared up the various tales, which had reached the aerodrome of our doings down at Hornchurch.

A 'phone-call to my wife to tell her to pack for forty-eight hours leave and then lunch. I was drinking, my coffee afterwards when I espied through the window a little grey Lancia come up the drive, a golden head showing behind the wheel. Good show—my lady hadn't wasted much time! A hurried farewell and I dashed up to my room to collect my bag and then we were away.

It was only when I got into the car and we started off that I realised that I was feeling a bit tired: It was not altogether surprising since for ten days we had been getting up at 3.15 in the morning, getting to bed usually about 11 at night. On top of that we had done quite a bit of flying and fighting. It was rather like playing a strenuous game of tennis on a hot day. You don't realise how hot you are until you stop.

All too quickly leave came to an end and we returned to the Station to a rather inactive routine. Before long, however, the Hun began coming over at night and one flight stood by during darkness each night. On June 19th "B" Flight was on and sent up several aircraft to try to find these nocturnal raiders.

I was over in the Mess about 11 o'clock that night with S/L Pinkham, and we strolled outside in the garden listening to the rising and falling note of the raider's engines sounding high up amongst the stars. A Hun was just passing over the aerodrome as we stood drinking a late cup of coffee just before going to bed. Suddenly, high up above us, sounded a faint whistling noise which gradually grew and grew until it sounded like an express tram passing with its whistle open. "Whistling bomb," somebody remarked. Nobody seemed anxious to get under cover as they were more interested than anything else. The sound grew louder and then ended abruptly, as the bomb burled itself in the ground a mile or so south of the Aerodrome—as far as we could judge.

I remember hunching myself up a little and waiting for the explosion. No sound came, however—it was a dud! Suddenly, however, from behind the Mess, came four shuddering "Crumps," and the windows rattled. Those weren't duds!

The activity died down for a while, and since I was off duty I got into my car and went home. There was great excitement when I arrived, the family standing out on the lawn watching the searchlights and regarding the whole thing as rather interesting entertainment. Eventually we went to bed, and I had just put the light out and was drawing the blackout curtains aside, and opening the window, when I heard the unmistakable "Brrrp" of machine-gun fire. My wife was out of bed and beside me in a flash!

I looked out into the night and there to the south three searchlights were groping against the stars, trying to find the elusive raider. As I watched, they stopped and a silver object gleamed brightly in their beams. There was another sound of machine-guns and a brief flicker of flame showed from the Hun. Then two white puffs appeared behind his tail. For a moment I thought it was smoke, then I realised they were parachutes—the crew had baled out. Another flicker of flame came from the stricken aircraft, and then it heeled over and plunged earthwards, a trail of smoke and flame behind it. The searchlights held the target still, the "blue note" from the engines echoing in the sky until the aircraft disappeared behind the trees across the road. There was silence for a split second and then a reverberating explosion and huge flash, followed by a red glare which lit up the whole heavens. Death of a raider.

It was John who had been responsible for the destruction of this Hun. I heard the tale next morning. He had sighted his target in the searchlight beams and had attacked. In coming in close for the final burst he had himself been illuminated in one of the beams arid a good burst from the German rear gunner had sent his petrol-tanks up in flames. He managed to get out, but was rather badly burnt in doing so and he was not to return to the squadron for many months.

The sequel to this was that Wilf had been chasing the same Hun and had just closed into range and was about to fire when there was a flash just beside him and a Spitfire went up in flames. It was John—neither knew that the other was there!

Meantime Ball had also found a Hun illuminated by the searchlights and had chased his quarry for twenty minutes before he finally caught up with it. He had fired all his ammunition but could not be certain that he had got it, only seeing it disappear beneath him in a dive. The next morning brought confirmation that a Heinkel had crashed into the sea just off the coast in the position he had engaged his target. A good night's work.

The crew of John's Heinkel were brought to the Station and the officer who was the captain of the aircraft turned out to be a really nice chap—a gentleman. The same could not however be said of the rest of his crew. He was brought to the mess until the prisoners were taken away, and as young Leonard was away at the time given his room to have a shave and a wash. Leonard returned at breakfast time, and walked up to his room to get the shock of his life when he found a German officer at work with his own razor! I was perhaps even more surprised after tea when my wife arrived to have a drink in the Ladies' Room with me whilst I was talking to our prisoner, for he told me he recognised her! At first I thought I had misunderstood him, but it turned out that he had seen her in Germany before the war when she had been over there motor-racing.

A few nights later on, on June 26th, "A" Flight was standing by. There were quite a few Huns droning about down to the south, but it was not until just after midnight that we were called upon to go up.

I was lying on my bed in the dispersal hut listening to the snores of the luckier pilots who could sleep at any rate until I took off, when the 'phone rang beside my bed. I groped about and eventually found it.

"Take off!"

"O.K."

I tumbled off the bed and out into the night. Somewhere out in the darkness an engine started up, breaking the stillness of the night. I peered in front of me trying to pick out the blue exhaust flames which would show me where my aircraft was. As I picked it out a tender came rumbling past me out on to the aerodrome—the flare-path officer going out to light up for me to take off.

As I approached my aircraft, the fitter began to run up the engine, and I stopped for a moment to listen to the music of a Merlin at full throttle. There was something very impressive, almost awe-inspiring in that thundering roar, sounding much louder in the darkness now than in daylight.

The fitter throttled back and as the engine note died to a spluttering mutter I bent down and clicked home the leg straps on my parachute, shrugging my shoulders to get comfortable in the harness as I moved to the aircraft. A heave on to the wing, and I stepped into the cockpit, settled myself in the seat and did up the straps as the fitter handed them to me.

"O.K., sir?"

"O.K.," and the man jumped down to the ground.

Turning up the cockpit lights until their orange glow lighted all the instruments, I glanced round, checking the coolant and oil temperatures and oil pressure, before running up the engine myself and taxi-ing out. Everything O.K., and I jerked my thumb over my shoulder, waiting until a torch flashed from behind to tell me the crew were holding down the tail and I could open the throttle.

Slowly I opened up to maximum, checked the boost pressure and revs, and then pulled the lever back, waving my hand above my head as the crew came running back to the wing-tips. Another flash from the torch and I knew that the chocks in front of the wheels had been pulled away and I could taxi out.

Out in front of me showed the faint line of lights which was the flare path. I switched off the cockpit lights to see better and then flashed on my light asking permission to take off. An answering flash came from the first light and I slowly moved forward, turning until I was pointing up the glimmering line of lamps. A glance round the cockpit to make sure all was m order, and I opened the throttle, gathering speed into the black wall of the night ahead. The last light flashed past just after I left the ground and watching the blind flying instruments, I got the undercarriage up, reset the airscrew pitch and closed the radiator slightly.

My altimeter showed 1,500 feet as I glanced out of the cockpit to pick out the horizon, a faint demarcation showing where earth met sky. The canopy of stars overhead was crystal clear, and I reckoned the visibility was a good twelve miles. It was dark, but not quite a "blackout" night. There was quite a good horizon, so I hadn't to concentrate on flying by my instruments.

I switched on the R/T and called up the Controller. His voice came crackling back to me in the earphones: "Receiving you O.K. There are some Huns to the east of you."

I acknowledged the message and turned east, climbing towards a bank of cumulous cloud ahead. As I entered the clouds a suspicious searchlight came on and groped about, trying to pick me up. It was very eerie with the silver glow lighting up weird shapes of caves and tunnels inside the cloud. Apparently the searchlight crew below became satisfied that I was a friendly aircraft and switched off. As I came out of the top of the cloud, all was dark again save the stars overhead.

At 15,000 feet I flattened out and steered towards a group of searchlights obviously trying to pick up an elusive Hun. Cruising around just behind them I waited, peering at the beams in the hope that I might see a faint silhouette even if the E/A was not actually illuminated. For an hour and a half I followed various groups of searchlights, but without any luck; then a voice in my 'phones told me to come back and land. I turned and began to lose height, following the courses I was given until I was fairly near the aerodrome. Down to a thousand feet and I began looking round for the flare path. Over on my left a line of lights shone out. Good show, I was nearly home. Circling the aerodrome I flashed on the light for permission to land. An answering light shone out and I began my approach. Wheels down, throttle back a little, 120 m.p.h.— O.K., flaps down, and I turned at the downwind end of the flare path. A light glared out below me as the floodlight was switched on, lighting up half the aerodrome. I straightened up, losing height all the time, until my altimeter showed 100 feet. Opening the throttle a little I held the aircraft at that height until I judged I was approaching the hedge, and then throttled right back. About 50 yards short of the floodlight I opened the throttle a little and began to ease the stick back. There was a terrific bump—Blast! I had misjudged it—I was too low. I gave a burst of throttle to ease the aircraft down off the bounce, wondering if my undercart was all right. I had certainly hit the ground pretty hard! As I passed the floodlight there was a much softer bump and I was down. Running down the flare path the left wing began to sink—so the undercart couldn't take it! I wasn't altogether surprised! Lower and lower the wing sank, until the tip touched the ground, and the aircraft slewed round, the nose dug in and we came to a shuddering standstill.

I switched off and climbed out feeling furious with myself, and walked back towards the tender coming to pick me up. As it stopped, I climbed in and sank down in the seat feeling very tired. The flare path officer came up and climbed aboard.

"Bad luck. You certainly hit the ground a wallop!"

"You're telling me! I nearly swallowed my teeth!"

I sat back as we drove back to the huts, cursing myself. A fine example I was setting to the rest of the flight! A flight commander is supposed to be past that sort of thing.

Next morning the C.O. spoke to me. "Bad luck, that show of yours. I am not altogether surprised, though. You'd been flying all day and then on top of that a couple of hours at night—you were just too tired."

I got some comfort from that, but I still felt a "twerp!"

Chapter 9

'A' Flight Has Some Luck:
1 July 1940-23 August 1940

July and August came and went and the autumn was beginning to draw on, but still we had no action. The Blitz had begun down south, and we were beginning to wonder if we were going to miss it.

Up to this time the squadron had been going out each day to an aerodrome near the coast to carry out convoy patrols, etc. August 16th found us at Coltishall, basking in the sun and hoping some Hun would come in and give us something to do. Nothing much had been happening all day and as tea-time approached we tossed a coin as to which flight should go up to the Mess for tea first. I lost for "A" Flight, and we stayed there on the sunlit aerodrome until "B" Flight should return.

After about a quarter of an hour the telephone rang—the squadron was to return home. I told them "B" Flight was up at the Mess and asked whether we should go off by ourselves or wait for the others to finish their tea. "No"—"A" Flight was to go off now.

We took off and circled the aerodrome, climbing for height, then Woody's voice came through—"Climb to 15,000 feet. There might be some 'trade' for you on your way back." We set course and climbed up through the sunlit haze and broken cloud.

We flew on for some minutes until I judged we must be near the coast. Then, from behind a bank of cloud sailed five Heinkels—then another five, and another, and another! A steady stream of aircraft appeared from the cloud, reminding me of a huge chorus coming out on to the stage from the wings.

There must have been at least 150 of them, Heinkels and Me 110 fighters and way above showed twelve thin white pencils of smoke—the top escort.

The leader of the formation must have seen us a few seconds after I sighted his formation, for the Huns turned out to sea, thin trails of black smoke from their exhausts showing that they had opened their throttles wide and were on the run.

"Keep an eye on those b— above us," I ordered. Then, as the humour of the situation struck me "My God, what a windy bunch!"

We were overhauling the Huns fast and the rearguard of 110's turned back to meet us, blocking our way to the bombers. Damn! There were at least 20 of them.

The old excited feeling fluttered at the pit of my stomach. I remembered getting exactly the same feeling stepping into the boxing ring at school. Thoughts raced through my mind. How could we get to those bombers. I glanced up at the white trails far above us. They hadn't seen us or else they thought we were a decoy and wouldn't come down. Ahead the 110's were circling to meet us. I glanced back at Frankie, leading his section behind me to the left. Could one section hold off the fighters whilst the others streaked after the bombers? No—we would have to leave Heinkels and content ourselves with a crack at the fighters.

The leading 110 was abreast of us now turning to come in behind us. I wheeled left, Frankie taking his section in to meet him whilst I headed to cut off some of the others. A 110 turned and came straight at me from above, six streams of tracer spurting from his nose as he opened fire. Hm! Not a very experienced pilot, judging by the range at which he opened fire, and I turned my head to see his tracer going 50 yards behind me. As he flashed past, I stall-turned to come in behind him, the rest of the section breaking away, each picking out an opponent.

I dived after mine and as he turned left I pulled round inside him, got the deflection and pressed the firing button. No—dammit—I missed him and he pulled hard round and went underneath me. I turned again in time to see another Spitfire on his tail. A burst of tracer and the Hun went down in a dive—steeper and steeper and, finally, plunging vertically downwards, disappeared into the clouds far below.

Good—that was one down—he obviously couldn't pull out of that dive—the clouds were only a couple of thousand feet up.

Turning again I climbed up towards two more Huns getting into position behind one of them. As I got there he saw me and began twisting and turning this way and that whilst I strove to get my sights on and take a steady enough aim to fire. At last he was right in the centre of the sight, and I opened fire. One gun immediately stopped. Blast it! I wasn't out of ammunition yet—must be a stoppage.

It looked as if I was hitting the 110, but he still twisted in front of me and I broke away to get into a better position. As I did so, another Hun came round on my tail and we started circling in what the Germans so aptly term a "Kurvenkampf." The Spitfire had a much better turning circle and as I began to gain on him and come round towards his tail he broke away into the opposite turn. It was a silly manœuvre, as it brought me on to his tail almost at once and I fired the rest of my ammunition. He broke away below me and I lost him from sight.

Feeling rather annoyed at having had no luck, I dived away towards the clouds. Glancing behind me, the fight appeared to be almost over. Away to the right a 110 was diving homewards, a Spitfire turning away from behind him and heading back towards the coast. The clouds below came rushing up to meet me and suddenly the dazzling white vapour blotted out the sun and sky. Concentrating on the instruments, I dived on down, the cloud gradually getting darker as my height decreased, until below a different shade of grey told of the sea beneath. The cloud thinned abruptly and I was out in the clear.

It was very misty down here, and for a while I couldn't pick up the horizon. The artificial horizon had been upset in the dogfight and was not working. The altimeter showed 2,000 feet, and I could tell I was still diving fast by the sound of the airstream and the noise of the engine, without looking at the air speed indicator. I eased back the stick and looked at the "turn and' bank" indicator. I was in quite a steep turn. Pushing the stick over to one side I got the kite more or less straight and then a lightship appeared to my right. It looked rather unusual as it seemed to be floating at an angle of 45°! I still wasn't straight yet, and correcting still more until the ship was in a normal position I looked ahead and saw the line of breakers on the shore, and lined up my wings on this horizon. The beach and cliffs slipped by underneath and I recognised a town to the south. 270° should be just about right to get home, and resetting the gyro from the magnetic compass below it, I sat back and settled down on the course, idly watching the fields and lanes disappearing slowly beneath the wings. I felt contented. We had been on the job again, and after a couple of months inactivity it was like a tonic. I was annoyed with myself for not getting anything. My eye must be a bit out. Ah well—wait till we got back and saw "B" Flight's faces! This would teach them to go and have tea first!

A town came into view beside the engine—funny I didn't recognise it, and I should be over familiar ground by now. I circled, trying to pick out some features I knew. From the look of the country I knew I was somewhere south of the aerodrome, but I wasn't quite sure whether east or west. Just then I heard the ground station at the aerodrome calling another aircraft. Waiting until they had finished, I called up and asked for a course home.

On to the new course, and the countryside began to look more familiar. Another transmission for a check bearing and I knew where I was. The aerodrome appeared in front of me and I dived down across it and came in to land. All the rest of "A" Flight was down and were talking to Crastor, our Intelligence Officer round the tail of one of the aircraft. Several of "B" Flight, including the C.O. and Wilf, were also standing there asking questions and cursing their luck.

Wilf shook his head sadly. "Dammit, it isn't fair!"

We all laughed—at least "A" Flight did! I got hold of Crastor to ask how we had done. "Three certain and one probable," he answered.

Grumpy had one certain and a probable and Sgt Potter had a cert as well, and young Jock had got his first one. It was his that I had seen going down into the clouds. Sgt Potter's remark had the laugh when he was told his seemed a certainty all right. "Well, I knocked the port engine out of the wing and the nose as far as the windscreen fell off as well, but he might have got home with a hell of a draught in his face!"

Chapter 10

A Question of Ammunition: 24 August 1940

A week later saw the squadron in action again. On August 24th after lunch we were ordered off to the London area, as a covering patrol whilst other squadrons down there were refuelling after battling with the Boche. The C.O. was away at the time and I was elevated to the leading position. It was a typical summer's day as we took off and climbed away south. The sun caught the haze below, making it difficult to see the ground.

At 17,000 feet we were over the outskirts of the Metropolis, still climbing, and watching the sun for any tell-tale glints which would tell of enemy fighters.

Woody's voice came over the air to me.

"There is some 'trade' to the south-east of you."

"Message received and understood" As we turned towards the Estuary one of the rear look-out section called up—

"Ack-Ack fire ahead and above."

A pause, then—

"Aircraft on the port bow, above."

Looking in the direction indicated, I saw some gleaming specks a mile or two ahead and two or three thousand feet above us. I opened the throttle wider and began climbing hard after them. Glancing down, the glint of sun on water showed the position of the Thames.

The specks grew larger and resolved themselves into Me 109's, their yellow painted noses shining golden in the sunlight. Ahead and below them was a formation of Me 110s and in front of them again, the bombers.

1. Squadron Leader Brian Lane DFC.

Above: 2. Eileen Ellison, Brian Lane's famous wife, a pre-war racing driving champion.

Left: 3. Squadron Leader & Mrs Lane at the wedding of Flying Officer Frank Brinsden, circa 1941.

4. No 19 Squadron's pilots at Fowlmere during the Battle of Britain: From left: Squadron Leader Lane, Sergeant Potter, Sergeant Jennings, Pilot Officer Aeberhardt, Flight Sergeant Unwin, Flight Sergeant Steere, Flying Officer Brinsden, Flight Lieutenant Lawson, Flying Officer Haines, Pilot Officer Vokes, Flight Lieutenant Clouston & Flying Officer Thomas.

5. Flight Sergeant George 'Grumpy' Unwin DFM.

6. Post combat de-brief, September 1940 (from left): Squadron Leader Lane, Flying Officer Crastor, Flight Lieutenant Lawson, and Sergeant Lloyd.

7. Briefing: Squadron Leader Lane (fourth from left) studies the map and briefs pilots of 19 and 616 Squadrons at Fowlmere, September 1940.

8. Sergeant Jennings scrambles from Fowlmere, September 1940.

9. Sub-Lieutenant Giles Arthur 'Admiral' Blake of the Fleet Air Arm, who flew Spitfires with 19 Squadron in 1940; sadly he would become the unit's last Battle of Britain fatality.

10. Flying Officer Frantisek 'Dolly' Dolezal, a Czech pilot with 19 Squadron.

11. Sergeant David Cox, 19 Squadron's first Volunteer Reserve pilot.

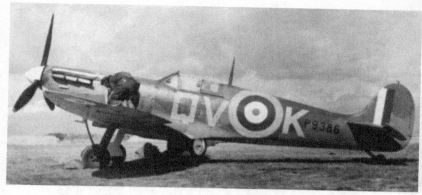

12. Brian Lane's Spitfire.

13. Squadron Leader Lane, facing the camera, immediately after a Battle of Britain sortie, with Flight Lieutenant Lawson and Flight Sergeant Unwin. The strain and exhaustion on the young Squadron Leader's face is all too evident.

14. Pilot Officer Wallace 'Jock' Cunningham DFC.

15. Armourer Fred Roberts removing ammunition tanks from Spitfire X4474, 'QV-I', flown by Sergeant Jennings.

Above: 16. Pilot Officer
Richard Jones of 19
Squadron.

Right: 17. Sergeant
Ken Wilkinson of 19
Squadron.

18. Sergeant Bernard 'Jimmy' Jennings of 19 Squadron.

19. Flying Officer Frank 'Fanny' Brinsden of 19 Squadron.

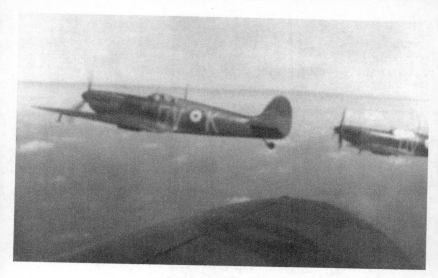

Above: 20. An extremely rare and very unofficial air-to-air photograph of Brian Lane, when commander of 19 Squadron's 'A' Flight, leading Red Section over East Anglia. The original was snapped by Pilot Officer Michael Lyne from the cockpit of Red Three. Red Two, as ever, is Flight Sergeant George 'Grumpy' Unwin.

Right: 21. Spitfire amongst the clouds.

22. Spitfire in flight over coast (Supermarine test pilot Jeffrey Quill in the first production Spitfire over Southampton, 1938).

23. Flight Lieutenant Brian Lane, wearing distinctive pre-war white flying overalls, pictured in his Spitfire Mk I at Duxford early in 1940 and whilst Commander of 19 Squadron's 'A' Flight. Interestingly the Spitfire has an armoured windscreen but no rear-view mirror. The swastika being shattered by a bolt of lightning bears the legend 'Blitzen' beneath, this being Lane's personal nose-art and carried on all of his Spitfires in 1940. This is the first photograph ever published on that hitherto unknown fact.

24. At the time of Munich.

25. Squadron Leader Brian Lane DFC, Commanding Officer of 19 Squadron, and the Squadron's mascot, 'Flash' the Alsatian, pictured by the Squadron Operations Caravan at Fowlmere during the Battle of Britain.

26. 'Flash' ready to scramble during the Battle of Britain wearing an iconic Irving flying jacket, B-type flying helmet and goggles!

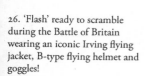

Above and below: 27. & 28. 'A' and 'B' Flight.

29. A Heinkel III.

30. Messerschmitt 109E.

31. Junkers (dive-bomber) 87.

32. Junkers 88.

33. A Dornier 215.

34. German fighter planes over France, photographed from the 34 Squadron-Commander's plane.

35. Part of a large formation of Heinkel III's, photographed with a fighter's camera gun.

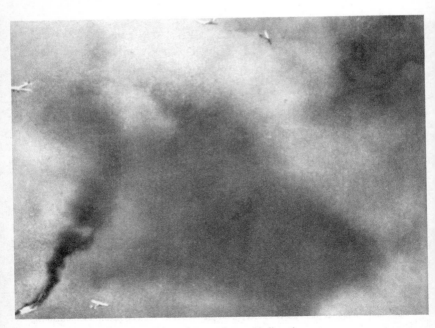

36. German plane crashing in aerial combat round coastal balloon barrage.

37. A parachute descent.

38. Hurricanes followed by Spitfires climbing to intercept.

39. Condensation trails from hundreds of German planes in a daylight raid.

40. A Dornier taken at close range in combat.

41. Five Heinkel 111's. The one on the right has its port engine on fire.

42. Spitfire-fly.

43. Flight-Sergeant Steere, Author, "Wilf" and Dolezal.

44. Sgt. Jennings, Author, "Flash," "Grumpy," F/Lt Colin McPhie, "Rangy", S/L Burton, Brinsden (on wing), and Leckrone.

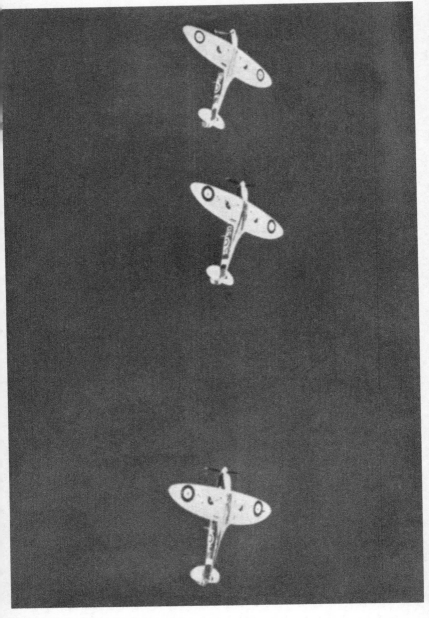

45. Spitfires on night patrol.

47. Pilots scramble to their Spitfires, June 1940.

48. A fighter pilot springs into action when the order comes, 1940.

Previous page: 46. 'Scramble'. From the alert relayed from a fighter station to the airfields fighters could be in the air within minutes. From the Battle of Britain Monument (Victoria embankment, London) sculptured by Paul Day.

49. Spitfires on patrol, 1940.

50. Hurricanes pulling away after making contact with German aircraft.

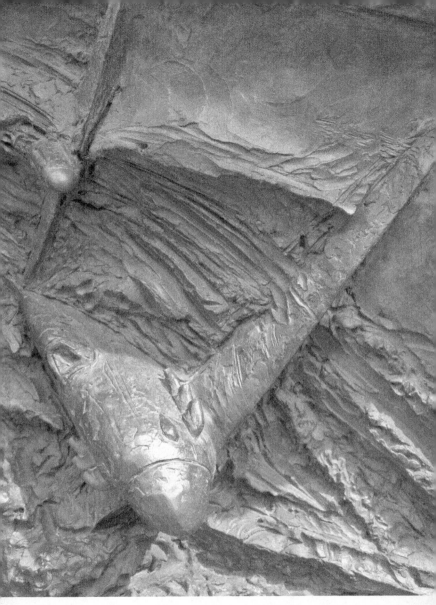

52. Air combat, a Spitfire pilot trying to avoid cannon shells fired from an Me 109 on his tail. From the Battle of Britain Monument (Victoria embankment, London) sculptured by Paul Day.

Opposite: 51. A fighter pilot with R/T equipment. From the Battle of Britain Monument (Victoria embankment, London) sculptured by Paul Day.

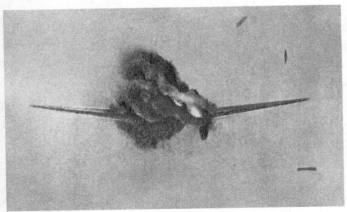

53. & 54. British gun-camera images of German aircraft being shot down.

Above: 55. The Battle of Britain was very visible to the British from the ground with swirling vapour trails marking the dogfights in the summer skies of 1940.

Right: 56. A doomed German Dornier 17 bomber aircraft plummeting earthwards after being attacked by British fighters.

57. A downed Me 109. This was the Luftwaffe's main fighter.

58. A downed He 111.

59. The young Brian John Edward Lane, whilst growing up in Pinner, Middlesex.

60. Pilot Officer Brian Lane pictured whilst flying Gloster Gauntlet biplane fighters with either 66 or 213 Squadrons before the Second World War.

61. A formal studio portrait taken at the time of Brian Lane's DFC was awarded for his leadership of 19 Squadron during the Dunkirk air-fighting - after the Commanding Officer, Squadron Leader Geoffrey Stephenson, had been shot down and captured during the Squadron's first engagement.

62. Flight Lieutenant Brian Lane pictured with his famous wife, the glamorous motor-racing champion Eileen Ellison.

63. An officer and a gentleman: Brian Lane in civilian clothes.

64. Squadron Leader Brian Lane, posing in flying helmet and oxygen mask, whilst serving briefly in the Western Desert in 1942.

65. Squadron Leader Brian Lane whilst serving at RAF Middle East HQ in 1942. Unfortunately Lane was unsuited to the climate and posted home in June 1942. Six months later he was reported missing in action whilst leading a completely useless sortie over the Dutch coast.

Twelve Spitfires slid in under the 109's and crept up towards the 110's in front. It was obviously out of the question to get to the bombers as they were too far ahead.

The only thing to do was to wade into the 110's, of which there were about two squadrons. As we got into range I singled out a target and the rest of the formation spread out and followed in. I opened fire from almost astern and the Hun went into a steep turn. As I followed him I noticed a stream of tracer apparently going straight into him. For a moment I thought it must be from another Spitfire, but suddenly realised that it was coming just over the top of my cockpit from behind me! My heart missed a beat.

Pulling sharply round out of the way I found another 110 on my tail. How he got there I don't know for I certainly did not see any of the Huns break formation until I opened fire. Keeping in the turn I got away from this gentleman, and feeling rather like a replica of that famous petrol advertisement, "That's Shell, that was!" had a good look round. Nobody seemed to be after me and I turned in after a 110 ahead, coming in from the side at him. I got a good sight on him and fired a long burst until a large portion of his port engine came right out of the wing. He lurched over on his side and fell half inverted towards the glistening water far below. Keeping a good look round, I managed to watch him on his last journey and was rewarded by the sight of a huge splash of white foam as he hit the sea just off the coast.

The fight seemed almost over now, for to the east a few aircraft were heading for the Belgian coast and a Spitfire was diving back towards home. No—there was nothing more to do but go back to the aerodrome. Then, as I turned north, a solitary 110 flew slowly past, half a mile away. Diving down a little I turned in under his tail and closed in behind him. Where he had suddenly appeared from I couldn't think, but the reason he was limping home so slowly was obvious now—

his starboard engine was out of action and I could plainly see the three blades of the stationary airscrew standing mutely out from the bulge of the engine. Throttling back and somehow feeling a bit of a cad, I took very careful aim, checked the range, and. pressed the firing button. Nothing happened.

I pressed it again. No—I was out of ammunition! Sitting there just behind him I swore softly to myself. The German pilot was obviously quite oblivious of my presence. What a shock he would have got if only I had had some ammunition!

Sliding out to one side I pulled up over the top of the E/A in a barrel roll, looking down through the roof of my cockpit as the aircraft became inverted. I laughed as I caught a glimpse of a pink blur in the front cockpit as the pilot looked up and saw me. He must have had the fright of his life!

Slipping down the other side of him I rolled out right way up, looking hard at the rear cockpit. The sliding cover was closed. If there was a gunner on board he must be dead.

I noticed the pilot had opened up his one good engine wide and a thin trail of black smoke was streaming back from the exhaust. I think he must have thought I was playing cat and mouse with him and I suddenly felt sorry for him. I could visualise his feelings as he strove to get away in his crippled aircraft, expecting at any moment to hear the clatter of bullets striking the fuselage and wings and waiting to feel one plough through his body.

I climbed and turned across his nose, rocking my wings as I straightened up and flew away from him. He would get home all right as long as he didn't over-rev that engine. Good luck to him, anyway.

And all the way back I pondered on my feelings. Why should I have felt sorry for that German pilot? War is war and no quarter is expected or given and yet, once the heat of the moment was over, I felt almost glad that I had been forced to give him that quarter. How contrary is human nature!

Tomorrow; perhaps, he would be on another raid in another machine and might shoot down one of our chaps, perhaps one of my flight, perhaps he might come upon me gliding home with a dud engine, and finish me off. I wondered if he would feel the same way I did, or whether the Nazi doctrine had killed all his decent feelings. Somehow I hoped it hadn't. Paradoxically in a fight I always hoped the other chap was a decent sort of guy. It was so clean up there in the blue—the thrill of flying and the bigger thrill of fighting—.

And yet if I had had some ammunition left I couldn't have missed him and I would have shot him down. "Cold meat!"— and I would have done it, not because I hated that German personally—I didn't know who he was—but because I wanted to and got a kick out of it. But if we had not been at war could I delight in killing? No. Sanity would prevail and we should all become once more normal people. Yet that German pilot was fighting for the filthy regime which had caused the war. He probably believed in it and admired its teachings.

Damn the stupid fool for being taken in by the lies and corruption which had been poured into his ears. God! if only I had had some ammunition!

Chapter 11

Sad Promotion:
25 August 1940-13 September 1940

August drew to a close and. then on September 5th the squadron came home without the C.O. I didn't go off with the squadron that morning as I only came back from leave as they were returning. Young Leonard had got a 109, F/O Walter 'Farmer' Lawson (promoted to F/L later this day) had a probable Dornier, and Sgt Plzak, our Czech pilot, had also got a probable 109.

Wilf rang through to the Operations Room asking for news. No news had come through yet.

"He's probably baled out," said someone.

"Hope so. Who saw him last?"

"I saw him heading into the middle of a bunch of 215's by himself. They must have got him—cross fire, probably."

The day wore on and then at tea-time came the news that the C.O.'s body had been found. He had apparently got out of his aircraft but was too low or too badly wounded to open his parachute.

A gloom descended on the Mess and there wasn't quite so much talking and laughter as usual as we sat drinking after supper that night.

Next day, after lunch F/O J.R Budd, our Adjutant, rang me up.

"Keep this under your hat until Woody rings up, but you've got the squadron. Congratulations."

"Shut up and stop blathering," I said.

"No, really. After all, you've had the ruddy squadron once before so I suppose they think you might as well try to make a mess of it again!"

"I don't want any of your rudeness, Budd," I said coldly,

using his surname. He laughed.

"Good lord, I shall have to salute you now, I suppose!"

"You're darned right! Has Frankie got 'A" Flight, then?"

"No—Lawson It's a bit tough, but after all he's had a good deal more experience."

He rang off and I went back to the tea-table. As I sat down—

"I am awfully sorry about this, Frankie, but I'm a ruddy squadron-leader and Lawson goes up to flight-lieutenant and takes the Flight. I am sorry—but it's just a question of experience, you see."

Frankie took it very well, although I knew he was disappointed. He had been my deputy ever since Dunkirk and when Lawson came in and was told the news Frankie congratulated him as sincerely as anybody.

Drinks that night were on Lawson and me. He took the promotion in his usual quiet way. He would make a darn good flight commander and he couldn't have a better deputy than Frankie.

On September 7th, the squadron went off on two patrols, the first at 11.25 being fruitless, no E/A were seen. We were operating in a wing again of three squadrons led by S/L D.R.S. Bader with his Canadians. The Czech squadron followed them and we were the top covering squadron, having a better performance than the two Hurricane squadrons.

In the afternoon shortly after tea, we were off again, flying in the same formation as in the morning. Climbing south we reached 7,000 feet when a large formation of about 200 bombers and fighters was intercepted. They were flying east towards the coast and the wing turned after them and climbed into the enemy formation. We were suffering from a disadvantage in height, and it looked as if only the Hurricanes would be able to get into range as we were too far behind.

High above the squadron was the top layer of the fighter escort, Me 110's and 109's. I began to climb up in an endeavour to get to them. As I did so a 110 came screaming down just in front of me, a Hurricane on its tail. As the aircraft passed the Hurricane broke away. Breaking up the squadron into sections I opened the throttle and tore after the Hun with my section. As we closed in behind him, four Hurricanes descended on him as well! Seven to one—most unfair! But the rest of the Huns were out of reach. It didn't take very long although the German pilot fought us off magnificently before he and his gunner baled out and their aircraft crashed in flames into a field. I watched the crew land near the burning wreck, and apparently taken prisoner by a maid from an adjoining country house, and then climbed up again in the hope that there might be some fun still about. The sky seemed to be empty, the Huns, the Hurricanes and even the rest of my section had disappeared. I heard Wilf calling up the ground station and asking where the party had gone to. I called him up and told him I was in the same boat, I had lost everybody too.

We got instructions to land and came back to the aerodrome. The rest of the squadron had had more luck than we had.

Young P/O W. 'Jock' Cunningham had got a He 111 in flames and damaged another. Grumpy had got two 109's and Dolly, the squadron's ever-smiling Czech, had got a 110. Not so bad, after all—four down and no loss to ourselves. The bag for the wing was 20 altogether for one or two casualties. Our arithmetic was getting better and better!

Two days later the wing was in action again, a party I unfortunately missed as I was not flying that day—and the total bag rose to 29, again for a negligible cost on our side.

Lawson got a Dornier, the 'Admiral' (Sub-Lieut Giles Blake) a Heinkel—and a bullet through his windscreen!—Jock a 109, and Frankie a Heinkel. The total squadron bag was now 50 certain and 18 probables, for the cost of four killed and one prisoner of war.

September 11th, and we took off and joined up with two other Spitfire squadrons to make up the wing. Again we were to act as a covering patrol over the London area.

Thirty-six Spitfires climbed towards the afternoon sun. I was leading the show and it felt like old times looking back at the formations behind me.

At 22,000 feet I turned east and flew along the Thames watching to the south for any trade which might be about. I had been told over the R/T that a raid was coming in towards the Capital.

As I looked a cluster of black mushrooms of smoke appeared at about 20,000 feet two or three miles away. It was the South London guns opening up. I called up the ground station and the rest of the formation as I sighted a swarm of aircraft in the middle of the Ack-Ack and turned to meet them. It was the sort of interception a pilot dreams of. We were going for them head on from slightly above. Behind the bombers I could see the fighter escort stepped up in layers above their charges; and they couldn't touch us until after we had carried out the first attack on the bombers!

I called up again on the R/T, and then we dived on the 12 leading Heinkels. I took the right hand Hun, the rest of the flight each picking out a target so as to cover the whole front of the formation. Down we went, rushing to meet them at something like 500 m.p.h., with the combined closing speed. A fleeting burst of fire and we were into them.

I think it must have shaken those Huns a lot. It must have been rather frightening to see the Spitfires rushing to meet them apparently in a head-on collision, Forty-eight guns of the leading flight spanning the space between with white pencils of tracer.

I held on to the last minute and then ducked to one side as a huge dark green monster flashed past. I caught an impression of the whirling airscrews, a black cross outlined in white, a gun in the rear cockpit swinging after me, a pink blur of the gunner's face showing behind it. Then they were gone.

I turned hard round to the left to come back. To my utter astonishment almost every aircraft had disappeared. Above me the flash of the sun on wings told of a dog-fight going on. No doubt the fighter escort and the rest of the Spitfires, but of what must have been over 50 bombers not one could I see! Nor could I see the rest of the flight, much less the Squadron!

Then towards the river I saw seven Heinkels turning for home, dropping their bombs as they turned: the leading bombers which we had attacked. There didn't seem to be much to stop them going on to the centre of London if they wanted to—only me! But no—they looked to have had enough and were going home. Well, we seemed to have got five of them down in that first 'attack—probably the leader had gone down and these other lads were lost and didn't know quite what to bomb. Anyway, they were on the run.

I turned after them, scanning the sky all the time for signs of fighters. Two Me 109's swam into view and joined up one each side of the bombers. They made no attempt to interfere with me, one of them merely dropping back behind the Heinkels. I closed in and fired at him from dead astern. I hit him with the first burst, a shower of pieces flying off from his starboard engine as the airscrew stopped. He made no attempt to avoid my fire, he just flew straight on. Puzzled, I broke away as I overshot him and turned to come back m again. Taking a sight on the port engine I opened fire again. At the second burst a huge cloud of smoke and flame belched out and the aircraft slowly went down in a dive. Breaking away I glanced down but he was lost from view. Looking back at the other aircraft I was amazed to see the remaining Me 110 diving away as hard as he could for home!

I obviously couldn't catch him, and anyway the bombers were more important to knock down. The Heinkels had tightened up their formation and were steaming along as fast as they could. I picked out the rearmost aircraft and then frowned. There were only six! I counted them again. Definitely six. I looked round but there was not another aircraft to be seen in the sky. Where the other Heinkel had gone I don't know to this day. When I broke away from the 110 I temporarily lost sight of the bombers, and it must have been then that he broke away or was possibly shot down by Ack-Ack.

I closed in behind the last Hun and eased the sights on to one of the engines and fired. I stopped for a moment to steady my kite in the slipstream and then fired again. Nothing happened.

Breaking away I climbed up to one side of the formation and came down in a beam attack on the leader. Still nothing happened. No return fire came from the Huns at all. Their crews might have been dead for all the response I got to my attacks. Turning round again I closed in behind No. 6 and opened fire at his starboard engine. After a short burst a cloud of white vapour streamed out from below the engine. Ah! I'd got his radiator! I fired again but my guns stopped after a second—out of ammunition—but not before I saw flames and black smoke come licking out around the engine cowling.

I broke away above him and looking back saw there were only five Heinkels now. I could account for that—a thin streak of black smoke showed where No.6 had gone plunging down.

Feeling rather exhilarated on getting two down, I dived back across the Thames and headed for home and a glass of beer—it was too late for tea!

Chapter 12

Der Tag!
14 September 1940

September 14th saw the wing on two patrols, but no E/A were seen. Perhaps the Hun was saving himself for the morrow. I think this was actually the case for the next day saw the record bag of 185 Huns shot down—these only the certainties, the real total therefore probably even higher.

We carried out two patrols, the first, at 11.30 hours I very nearly missed as my aircraft refused to start. After about ten minutes my fitter managed to get it going and as two other aircraft had just been made serviceable I took off with a section consisting of the Admiral and Jock.

We climbed away south as hard as we could without much hope of catching up with the wing. At 20,000 feet just over the outskirts of London I sighted some Ack-Ack fire ahead. We were luckier than I had even hoped, for as we drew nearer I saw a loose formation of about 15 Domiers with several 109's above them. They were flying west and it looked as if the wing had already been at them, as in fact they had.

Keeping an eye on the 109's, which apparently hadn't seen us, I turned in from ahead of the formation and dived at the leader, the Admiral and Jock picking a target each side of me.

We weren't quite dead ahead of the E/A and coming in at a slight angle I misjudged the deflection when I opened fire, the bullets going behind the Dornier. I flashed through the formation and pulled up in a climbing turn as a 109 came down on me. He came at me from the side and dived straight on underneath me and disappeared. Where he went to I don't know—he may have been out of ammunition and going home.

The sky was clear above the sun shining down from the blue of the heavens on to the dazzling layer of cloud 10,000 feet below us, the Dorniers standing out starkly black against the snowy whiteness. As I came round behind the formation again I saw the Admiral's aircraft behind one of the E/A and marked the white streaks from the wings as he opened fire—then I was closing behind my own target.

I came in rather fast and fired a short burst as the aircraft bumped in the bomber's slipstream, breaking away hard down below the twin rudders as they seemed to rush almost into the cockpit. Pulling out of the half loop I began to turn again towards the enemy formation when I saw a Dornier diving past me going east. Reversing the turn I followed, firing from the quarter at the starboard engine. As I slipped in astern of the Hun a Hurricane swam up beside me firing also. I turned away to one side and saw two more Hurricanes behind him. Dammit! Who saw this Hun first?

Then I realised that the Hurricanes had probably been chasing this Dornier when I had come in and attacked. Perhaps after all I was horning in on them! I looked back to see if there was anything else about. No—the sky was empty save for the Hun, the Hurricanes, and me.

Taking my place in the queue I waited my turn to fire! The German pilot seemed to be taking no evasive action at all, the Dornier just diving slightly towards the clouds. Getting impatient I pulled out to one side and began a quarter attack aiming at the starboard engine again. This time I think I hit him, but it may have been one of the Hurricane pilots who was firing at the same time, as the E/A began to dive more steeply and s it went through a hole in the clouds, two white mushrooms blossomed forth as the wretched Huns baled out. The pilot was probably dead, as only two parachutes were floating down. Throttling back I dropped one wing to get a better view of the black-crossed aircraft. Behind, rushing over trees and hedges, fields and roads to meet the stricken machine, I saw its shadow. As the two came nearer and nearer a house loomed up, apparently in the path of the raider. With a sigh of relief I watched it miss the obstacle and then shadow and master met with a huge gush of flame as the aircraft hit the ground and the petrol-tanks exploded. I circled, watching the pillar of black smoke rising up towards the clear blue sky above to mark the grave of another of Goering's pride. Turning back I saw the two white shapes of the parachutes as the rest of the crew floated down. One landed in a field and then I was on top of the other. I saw the black figure at the end of the shroud lines gesticulating violently and felt tempted to give him the burst he was so obviously expecting. Anger surged up inside me as I remembered the unbroken layer of cloud over London through which these "brave" Huns had been shovelling their bombs! Looking back I saw the parachute swinging violently in my slipstream only a few feet from the top of a wood and laughed—

I hope that breaks your neck, you bloody little swine!

The morning's party was only a very small foretaste of what was in store after lunch. The sun was only just past the zenith when we were in the air again, forming up in the usual wing formation. As we climbed away towards London, S/L Bader, Woody and I exchanged wisecracks as we usually did on the way to our patrol line, in between more serious messages.

The weather was fine, the golden blaze of the sun high in the blue picking out the fleecy layer of clouds far below us. At 20,000 feet a message came crackling through in my 'phones—Woody's calm familiar voice saying, "There's some trade heading N.W. to the south of you."

"Lovely," came from Ball in reply and then ahead some black puffs of smoke showed up a myriad black specks. Huns and plenty of them!

The old feeling fluttered again at my stomach as I settled myself more comfortably in my seat, tested the reflector sight, which I knew perfectly well was working O.K., and glanced round at the rest of the squadron.

Looking back again at the rapidly growing black specks I saw above them a tangle of white condensation trails—the whole sky ahead seemed filled with aircraft. As we got closer I recognised the bombers as Dorniers, about 30 in each formation stretching away towards the coast to the south. Above the bombers weaved Me 109's and 110's, the escort. Never before, or since, have I seen so many enemy aircraft in the sky at one time. There were literally hundreds of them! It was an amazing sight and one which I shall remember all my life—it made the mass fly past at the Hendon Display seem small by comparison. It must have been about the maximum effort of the Luftwaffe.

As we climbed as hard as we could towards the Huns, the leading Dorniers crossed our bows and headed away to our right with their attendant escort.

I kept glancing up at those white trails just above, a gleaming speck at the head of each showing the fighters themselves. As we headed across the stream of aircraft I heard Ball call up but I didn't catch what he said, then I saw him turn away into the nearest formation of bombers with the rest of the Hurricanes, whilst I continued up into the escort with the Spitfires to try and hold them off while the bombers were being attacked. Glancing at No.2 of my section, I noticed that he was just beginning to make a trail and looking up again as a 109 passed over the top of me I judged we were about 1,000 feet below them. I have never felt so uncomfortable in all my life; we were a perfect target and could do nothing save continue climbing into the fighters, waiting all the while to be attacked from the ideal position—above and behind. I didn't feel scared now, there was too much to occupy my attention, but my—sit-me-down" was twitching as if I was expecting someone to kick me there and all the time I was squinting up into the glare above trying to keep an eye on all those damned Huns.

Suddenly I caught sight of a flash in my mirror, and turned as a couple of 109's came down on the rear section of the squadron. We opened out and after a few seconds split up as we swam up into the middle of a whole horde of 109's and 110's.

Why they hadn't attacked before I cannot think, but probably their idea was to draw us up into them to distract our attention from the stream of unescorted bombers which I later found were following at intervals behind the leading mass of aircraft. It almost seemed as if they hadn't sufficient fighters to escort all the bombers they sent over.

Ahead of me was a squadron of Me 110's and after a quick look round to see that no other Huns were immediately concentrating on me I climbed up after the rearmost 110. Unfortunately, before I could get close enough to fire they saw me and paid me the compliment of all forming a defensive circle! Remembering the pilot who managed to get inside one of these circles going round in the opposite direction and keeping the firing button pressed as the string of targets passed through his sights, I decided now was the time to do likewise. But for the fact that I was now below the Messerschmitts I think I might have succeeded, but as it was I couldn't get into the middle of them quickly enough and was forced to break away as the leader came round behind me. As I straightened out again and began to climb up, a pair of 109's descended on me, but I managed to sidestep, so to speak, and they passed harmlessly to one side and pulled up in a climb ahead of me. As I opened the throttle wide and climbed after them they did a very foolish thing. The leader turned left and No.2, instead of following him, turned away in the opposite direction, right across my nose.

He saw me as I turned after him and putting on full inside rudder as he turned, skidded underneath me. Pulling round half stalled, I tore after him and got in a short burst as I closed up on him again before he was out of my sights again. That

German pilot certainly knew how to handle a 109—I have never seen one thrown about as that one was, and I felt certain that his wings would come off at any moment. However, they stayed on, and he continued to lead me a hell of a dance as I strove to get my sights on him again. Twice I managed to get in a short burst but I don't think I hit him, then he managed to get round towards my tail. Pulling hard round I started to gain on him and began to come round towards his tail. He was obviously turning as tightly as his kite could and I could see that his slots were open, showing that he was nearly stalled. His ailerons were obviously snatching too, as first one wing and then the other would dip violently.

Giving the Spitfire best, he suddenly flung out of the turn and rolled right over on his back passing across in front of me inverted. I couldn't quite see the point of this manœuvre unless he hoped I would roll after him, when, knowing no doubt that my engine would cut whereas his was still going owing to his petrol injection system, he would draw away from me. Either that or he blacked out and didn't realise what was happening for a moment, for he flew on inverted for several seconds, giving me the chance to get in a good burst from the quarter. Half righting himself for a moment, he slowly dived down and disappeared into the clouds still upside down, looking very much out of control.

The sweat was pouring down my face and my oxygen mask was wet and sticky about my nose and mouth. I felt quite exhausted after the effort and my right arm ached from throwing the stick round the cockpit. At speed it needs quite a bit of exertion to move the stick quickly and coarsely in violent manœuvres.

Looking round, the sky seemed empty and I dived down to follow the 109 and see if he had crashed or whether I could find him and finish him off if not. As I reached the top of a cloud layer I noticed away to the west a formation of about 20 aircraft flying south-east.

Climbing up again as hard as I could I got up into the sun above them and waited until they approached beneath me. They were Dorniers again, with no escort. Before I came down on them I had a good look round but could see nothing else in the sky at all.

I don't think they saw me until I was on top of them and what tracer did come from the rear guns was not very close to me. I fired at the leader in a quarter attack but with the speed of the dive I couldn't get in a very long burst and had to break away quickly underneath the formation, rolling over and pulling out in the opposite direction to that in which they were flying. As I pulled out, there in front of me was another formation of about the same number of Dorniers.

I was in a fairly good position for a head-on attack and since this seemed to be about the only way I could break up a formation of this size by myself, I sailed in at them. As I fired at the leader I saw the aircraft on his right wobble a bit and wondered whether my bullets weren't going quite where I thought they were, or whether the pilot just didn't like the look of a Spitfire coming at him head on.

The Huns rushed to meet me, and I remember involuntarily ducking my head as the leader's port wing flashed over the cockpit, then I was through the formation and turning back after them again.

Far from breaking up the formation, my efforts seemed to have had the opposite effect as the Dorniers had closed up until they were flying with their wings almost overlapping. Those Huns certainly could fly in. formation and since there wasn't enough room to get through them again from the front, I pulled up to one side, got slightly ahead of the leader and then came down in a beam attack. I was certain from the sight and the tracer that my burst hit at least one other aircraft, if not the leader, but there was no visible effect, they just sailed on towards the coast.

Breaking away behind them I noticed that the last man on the starboard flank of the formation was straggling a little. A steep left hand turn and I came in behind him firing at one engine. I heard a sharp metallic bang and then my guns stopped. I broke away as obviously I was out of ammunition, and that bang I had heard was obviously a bullet from the German rear gunner. I quickly glanced over all the engine instruments but all was well—he hadn't hit the engine.

A last regretful glance after the Dorniers and I turned for home, feeling rather annoyed at not getting any of those bombers. I was sure I had been shooting straight—they must be carrying a lot of armour on them these days—Blast them!

Ah well—"Home James," and find out how the others fared.

Back on the deck once more everyone was busy over their combat reports, Crastor fussing round getting the score as he collected the completed forms, and a good score it was too. Twelve certain and five probables. Sgt H.A.C Roden had got a bullet in his engine and had forced-landed, and Sgt Potter was missing—these were our only casualties. Young Leonard had excelled himself and got three certain, two 109's and a 110, and Grumpy had got three as well, all 109's. Grumpy with some 109's always reminded me of a terrier amongst rats! Of the others, Sgt D.G.S.R. Cox had got a 109, F/Sgt Steere a Dornier certain and a 109 probable, and Wilf a 110 and a Dornier both certainties, and Jock and the Admiral each a 109.

Of the rest of the wing, S/L Bader hadn't been quite so lucky, as his squadron and the Czechs close behind had been jumped on before we could get into the escort and hold them off, but for all that they had done well, the Czechs also having a good bag. The total for the day for the wing amounted to 52, our own casualties being covered on the fingers of one hand. That night the sun was blood red as it sank beyond the Western horizon.

Chapter 13

Out of Control:
15 September 1940-27 September 1940

The Blitz was not yet over, but September 15th saw the climax of it. Activity continued, however, on a fairly heavy scale for several days, and the wing carried out at least one patrol almost every day. On the 18th of the month we went off three times, and the first two patrols yielding nothing, I decided I might go over to my office to get on with a bit of work.

I was there when shortly after four o'clock the wing was ordered off again. Jumping into my car which I always had with me for these occasions, I tore round to dispersal point just in time to see 12 Spitfires taxi-ing away down the aerodrome. Some cad had taken my aircraft! It didn't matter from the operational point of view, as Wilf used to lead when I was away at any time, but I was furious at getting left behind. At the same time I couldn't help smiling and remembering another instance when a flight commander found his aircraft unserviceable and ordered another pilot over the R/T to give up his kite, whereat the latter developed mysterious R/T failure until he was in the air! It showed a grand spirit, and I could hardly imagine such a thing happening in a German squadron.

Alternately swearing and smiling to myself I repaired to the Operations Room, there to watch the progress of the wing. Woody, as usual, had come from his office to takeover and very unsympathetically roared with laughter when I told him why I was there.

As luck would have it this third patrol which I had missed was the one in which the wing got into a party, a large formation of Heinkels, Junkers 88's and Me's being sighted east of London.

I made my way back to dispersal point as the aircraft returned and waited with Crastor for the pilots to taxi in. From their faces it was quite obvious that they had had some fun. Out of the total for the wing of 28, the Squadron had accounted for six plus one probable. Wilf had got a Ju 88, Haines shared a Ju 88 and a probable 109; Dolly and Sgt Plzak, our Czech pilots, each a He 111, and Grumpy (as usual) had added to his score with a Me 110. F/Sgt Steere had also got a Heinkel and shared a Ju 88 with Haines, and Lawson and his section had polished off another Ju 88 between them. Unfortunately Lawson had had to force-land at Eastchurch aerodrome with a bullet in his coolant tank. News came through that he was quite O.K., however, to our relief. Two days later came the news that Grumpy had got the D.F.M. We were all very pleased about it.

September 22nd was a dirty day, low rain clouds obscuring the sun. Taking advantage of this, a Dornier paid us a visit, dropping a stick of bombs along "B" Flight's dispersal point. They were only small bombs and apart from blowing one of the aircraft up on its nose and filling the cockpit with earth, no damage was done. Lawson had taken off with his section just before this to try and intercept the raider and caught him over the aerodrome, getting in a burst before the Hun got back into the clouds again.

Five days later the wing was on patrol south of London and intercepted a formation of Me 109's. The Hun by now had almost completely given up large-scale bombing raids, contenting himself instead with sending over 109's on offensive sweeps, some of these fighters carrying bombs in order to increase their nuisance value more than anything else, I think, judging by the results they obtained.

We were flying south-east at the time and some bursts of

A.A. fire ahead showed us a formation of about twenty or thirty 109's flying north in loose formation. As they saw us they turned to meet us and S/L Bader waded into them, the rest of us following. As the squadron broke up, I noticed two yellow-nosed Huns creeping round underneath us to try and attack from below and behind.

Half rolling I dived down on them, getting in a short burst at each of them as they passed through my sights. I was coming down rather fast in the dive and felt the aircraft skidding slightly. My left hand felt for the rudder bias control and wound the wheel back. Still the aircraft continued to skid and trying to pull out of the dive I found that I couldn't. I was doing a fair rate of knots and the controls had stiffened up a great deal accordingly, but a backward movement of the stick did not have the customary effect! Pressing as hard as I could on the left rudder pedal had little or no effect either, as it was almost impossible to move it at this speed.

A glance at the airspeed indicator showed me I was doing well over 400 m.p.h. and the altimeter was giving a good imitation of one of those indicators you see in lifts. To say that I. was a trifle worried about all this would be a slight understatement. I had started this blasted dive at 25,000 feet and the altimeter now showed 10,000. I was just beginning to think about stepping out, and then began wondering whether I could at this speed. I decided to have one last attempt at getting control.

Bracing myself against the back of the seat I put both feet on the left pedal and pressed as hard as I could, pulling back on the stick at the same time. Relieved was hardly the word, as I felt the aircraft straighten up and saw the nose rising to meet the horizon. Determined to make no mistake about pulling out of the dive completely, I kept the stick back and not unnaturally blacked out completely as the controls regained their full effect.

Easing the stick forward again I came to and was confronted with the sight of a parachute upside down and apparently ascending instead of descending. Further examination of this phenomenon drew my attention to the fact that the sun was below me! I had completed a half loop while I was blacked out without knowing it.

I rolled out right way up and circled round the white mushroom of silk, trying to recognise the pilot at the end of the shroud lines. High above me one or two aircraft were still circling round but the dog-fight seemed to be over. Circling round I waited until the pilot came to rest in the top of a tree and then diving down (slowly this time!), caught a glimpse of him climbing down to the ground. He was obviously O.K. and I couldn't help laughing at his predicament. As he reached the ground he waved, and I turned for home.

Back on the aerodrome I found out that it was Gordon who had taken to the silk. His machine had been set on fire and he had had to get out in a hurry. He had left us a couple of months ago to take over a flight in the Czech squadron.

Our score for the day was good. Seven 109's down plus one probable. Lawson, Potter, Steere, Grumpy and our Czech Sgt Plzak, had each got one, the Admiral had got two and Sgt Jennings had a probable—and I had had a fright! The trouble was later traced to a "bowed" rudder, and the rudder bias out of adjustment. This had prevented me from being able to trim the aircraft straight in the dive, the ensuing skid causing the rudder to blank off one side of the elevators, thus causing the effectiveness of this control to be greatly decreased. Later I went up to test the aircraft again and all was well, the faults having been remedied.

The same day we learned that Jock and Leonard had both got the D.F.C., and we had a celebration that night in the Mess to mark the occasion.

Chapter 14

Quiet Days:
28 September 1940-15 November 1940

It was obvious now that the Blitz was over and that at any rate for the time being the Luftwaffe had shot its bolt.

Enemy activity declined, offensive patrols by Me 109's, some carrying, bombs to increase their nuisance value, took the place of the mass bombing raids. As a result of this there wasn't enough trade to go round! And although the wing continued patrols whenever any enemy activity occurred in the Channel, it became obvious that we should have to be very lucky to get any more action. As It happened we did have a bit of luck, but not until November 5th.

On this occasion I was unfortunate in missing the patrol, Lawson leading the squadron. His R/T, however, became unserviceable shortly after taking off and F/Sgt Steere took over the lead. Over Canterbury a considerable amount of cloud was experienced, and the squadron became separated from the rest of the wing. Shortly afterwards a formation of 109's was sighted and attacked. The E/A dived into the clouds and disappeared, but not before Lawson had fired at one from 150 yards range and seen the cockpit cover break off. He fired again, giving a five-second burst, and the 109 disappeared in a vertical dive into the clouds and apparently crashed into the sea 10 miles south of Dungeness.

Sgt H.W. Charnock claimed his first victim since joining the squadron. He climbed up after three E/A which were circling 500 feet above him and after four turns got on the tail of one, the other two breaking away and disappearing from sight. Opening fire at the remaining Hun from about 200 yards he fired six bursts closing to 50 yards before breaking away to see the 109 with smoke and flame pouring from the engine.

In the afternoon Lawson again was lucky over the same area, running into another bunch of 109's and the new Heinkel 113's. This time he made certain of his opponent and had the satisfaction of seeing the E/A completely break up in the air after he had fired only about 20 rounds per gun. It was excellent shooting.

Grumpy also added another to his score, chasing a 113 across the Channel and catching it over the French coast. It was the first and only E/A of this type to be shot down by the squadron.

Unfortunately the squadron came back without P/O Hradil, one of our two Czech officers, and a report was later received that a Spitfire had been seen falling in flames over the Thames at the time of the fight: His body was never found and it obviously must have been poor Hradil who had been seen.

The next ten days were quiet, and although we carried out several patrols nothing was seen.

Then, on the morning of the 15th, two squadrons, S/L Bader's and ourselves, were sent off to patrol a convoy off the Estuary.

We climbed up towards the sun and set course over the banks of rolling mist covering the tree-tops. It was a glorious morning, the sun shining down from a cloudless blue sky on to the wisps of white vapour clothing the earth below.

Out to sea the mist had cleared a little and before long Bader picked up the convoy and began running up and down the line of ships.

Owing to the limited visibility he decided to patrol fairly low at about 7,000 feet, whilst I climbed up behind him to keep a look-out for any higher stuff that might come in.

Away to the south over the French coast a tangled mass of smoke plumes high up in the blue showed where some Huns were having a morning trip: It was not our job to chase them, however, so I sat back idly watching the white trails weaving a fantastic pattern against the heavens.

Glancing farther to the east towards Dunkirk I saw two more white plumes and watched to see which way the E/A were heading. They seemed to be coming our way.

Switching on my transmitter I called up Bader and told him I was going up higher in case the Huns should come within reach.

"O.K., pal," came back in my 'phones as I turned towards the trails. Climbing south I edged round towards the sun to try and take the Huns by surprise. There was about 10 miles separating the two aircraft and I called up Wilf and told him to break away with "B" Flight and take the rearmost one whilst I went after the other with "A" Flight. Up and up we climbed, and after a few minutes Wilf called up and asked if I could head his chap off a bit as they weren't gaining on him very quickly.

Telling Grumpy with his section to break away and try to cut off the Hun in question, I climbed on after the other one; at about 22,000 feet he passed over the top of us heading up the Estuary and I turned in behind getting between him and the sun.

At 25,000 feet I noticed that we were making condensation trails as well and began to wonder when our quarry would see us. We were still several miles behind him and at least 5,000 feet lower but I could now pick out the aircraft at the head of its white tail of smoke. I could see that it was a twin-engined kite but we weren't near enough yet to recognise the type.

The Ack-Ack batteries were firing at the E/A and I sat watching the white puffs of the exploding shells bursting below and behind him to come floating lazily back to meet us as we climbed on and on after him.

I began to think we were never going to catch up as we didn't seem to be gaining on the Hun to any great extent and it seemed as if our climbing speed was the same as his cruising speed. Accordingly I eased the stick forward a little until we were flying level and we began to catch up. As we got nearer, I began climbing slightly again trying to get the happy medium between maximum climb and forward speed.

We were now at almost 30,000 feet and over the outskirts of London. Apparently this was as far as the Hun wanted to go, for he turned slowly round the way he had come... and then he saw us and did a very foolish thing. He dived down as hard as he could back towards the sea.

As it was I turned and dived after him, Jock and P/O Arthur Vokes following in line astern. Down, down we went, the needle of the airspeed indicator going farther and farther round the dial until it showed 400 m.p.h.. In reality, our speed must have been nearly 500 m.p.h., as in the rarified air at these altitudes there is quite a large error of anything up to 100 m.p.h. in the instrument.

The controls were solid now with the force of the air flow over them, and it needed two hands and a lot of strength to move the stick even a little.

We were gaining on the Hun now and gaining fast, and at 10,000 feet I began to ease the sights on to the fuselage of the target. I say "ease' but perhaps heave would be a better word. I was sweating with the strain of holding my aircraft steady in the bumps as I began to get the Hun's slipstream. My head felt thick and I was almost deaf from the sudden change from the rarified atmosphere above to the increased pressure lower down.

At last I was in range and squinting through the sight. I pressed the firing button.

The muffled "Br-r-r-r-p" of the guns came to my ears as streams of tracer leaped from the wings and flashed towards the E/A in my sight. I fired three bursts steadying my aim between each and then pulling away to the left, a stream of black smoke coming from the port engine as I did so. Straightening up I watched Jock firing and then the starboard engine spluttered and a tongue of flame licked out around the cowling. Good show! Cunningham we've got him.

I watched Arthur close in behind the 110 and as broke away the E/A pulled up in a climbing turn and I closed in from the side and gave him another squirt. He turned over on his side and a parachute blossomed out behind as the burning aircraft dived through a patch of cloud and crashed in a huge fountain of white foam and steam into the blue waters of Father Thames.

We were now at 2,000 feet and watching until the German pilot had been picked up by a boat. I turned and called up the other two of the section, heading home over the carpet of mist still covering the land.

After a while I picked up a town through a gap in the mist and a few minutes later sighted a familiar landmark sticking up through the white vapour and came to the aerodrome.

Landing, I found that "B" Flight had accounted for the other E/A, which had also turned out to be a Me 110. The two were obviously on reconnaissance flights and it was nice to think that the Huns had lost two aircraft and a lot of photographs which they probably thought they could get without trouble.

Wilf's scheme for getting the second 110 had worked admirably and Grumpy had headed him off just as "B" Flight came up behind the quarry. Thus nine Spitfires had pounced on the wretched Hun at the same time and it was small wonder that he had not survived the encounter. He had dived headlong towards the sea in an effort to escape, the Spitfires streaming after him, and one wing had broken off before he hit the water. It was rather hard to say who had been most instrumental in getting him, as everyone except Wilf had fired.

Over a glass of beer before lunch I heard Wilf's account.

"The bastards just shouldered me out of the way;" he said indignantly. "I couldn't get near enough to fire at all!" Roars of laughter greeted this remark. That the flight commander, who was supposed to be leading the attack should be pushed aside, so to speak, by the rest of his flight, all determined to get in a burst, struck everybody as being extremely funny.

Chapter 15

The Day's Work:
16 November 1940-13 March 1941

We settled down now for the winter and a monotonous existence again, only alleviated by the fact that the days were shorter. Perhaps it might be well if I were to describe an average day in a fighter squadron at this juncture.

The squadron stands by from dawn until dusk. During winter this does not entail any great hardship, but during the summer months it means that the pilots are on duty perhaps seventeen hours each day.

Enemy activity to a fighter pilot is a tonic compared to long periods of enforced idleness. Once having tasted action, all other flying rather loses its meaning and tends to appear rather pointless.

Before the war I had read numerous books written by pilots about the last war, many of whom had never flown since the Armistice. It seemed extraordinary to me that anyone could give up flying once they had started, but now I begin to realise how they feel about it, and how we shall feel when the war is over and the sky will be empty of enemy aircraft. From habit we shall still keep peering into the sun looking for the tell-tale glint of a fighter above, knowing full well that no fighter will be there, and realising that a sense of futility is bound to creep in.

Fighting is the supreme goal towards which all our previous flying has been directed, and now we shall have reached that goal and the game will be over. We shall still enjoy flying for its own sake but it will seem insipid. Having tasted wine, water will not satisfy.

But I am digressing. When there is no enemy activity there is training flying to be done. New pilots must be taught the applied flying which they cannot learn anywhere else but in a squadron. The exerienced pilots must keep their hands in, new tactics must be evolved, night flying training carried out and so on. All this and in addition, as far as the C.O. is concerned, quite a lot of office-work.

After breakfast, then, if the Hun is quiet, the training flying commences and continues on and off all day. Good weather at dusk and some night flying probably rounds off the day's work. Except those down for flying, the remainder of the pilots are free until they come on duty again at dawn on the morrow.

A pilot doesn't get very much chance for relaxation except in the winter evenings, but plenty of leave is usually forthcoming and allows him the necessary mental and physical rest he requires.

Dud weather means boredom, which is bad for morale. Given something to do, particularly with the enemy, everyone is happy. Too much action is worse than boredom, of course, and when a pilot has had a "bellyful," away he goes to a flying school as an instructor for a rest from operational flying.

Every day of the week seems the same; Sunday is just another working day. At the beginning of the war I always felt rather lost and never knew what the date was, but after a while one gets used to it and it must be Sunday if the paper boy delivers the *Sunday Pictorial* instead of the *Daily Mirror*!

Leave brings temporary and welcome freedom. No longer does the ring of the telephone-bell control your life; but the Adjutant has got your address, and you might receive a telegram, "Return Unit Immediately;" should circumstances demand it. As a matter of fact, during the Blitz I found it very hard to get chaps to go on leave—they were all afraid of missing a chance of getting at the Hun!

Now, however, leave was eagerly looked forward to. The wing still carried out patrols in the hope of catching some 109's, and on November 28th a small formation was seen over Ramsgate and Lawson had a crack at them. The net result was three down, and no loss to the squadron, Leonard having got one certain, F/Sgt Steere another, and Grumpy and Sgt David Fulford sharing another. This was the last action the squadron was to have up to the time of writing, and brought the squadron score up to 91 certain and 30 probable, for our own casualties of under double figures. Although this score did not compare with those of other squadrons nearer the scenes of activity, at the same time we felt justly pleased with ourselves at arriving at that score with the loss of so few of our own chaps.

The old faces were, however, fast disappearing through postings to other units. Gordon and Ball had left us some time before to take over flights in other squadrons. Frankie soon followed them and then Wilf left to take command of a new squadron which was forming. Grumpy and F/Sgt Steere had also been posted from the squadron to become instructors. Wilf, Gordon Sinclair and F/Sgt Steere had all been awarded "Gongs" (medals to you!) after Dunkirk and Grumpy during the Blitz, to which was added a bar before he left us. Lawson and Jock were soon afterwards given the D.F.C., and then two old faces were welcomed back to the squadron in John and Michael. John took over "B" Flight after Wilf's departure, but although he showed himself to be an excellent flight-commander it soon became obvious that he hadn't fully recovered from his experience that night in June. He resolutely refused to admit it, and was furious when eventually he was posted away as an instructor to give him a rest from the cares and worries of a squadron and to give him a chance to get really on his feet again.

New pilots kept arriving to fill the vacancies left, some to be posted again to new squadrons just formed after we had trained them up. And so it went on. Sometimes a section would be sent off to try and intercept a solitary Hun snooping about in the cover of the clouds on days of bad weather, but it was like looking for a needle in a haystack.

And then one day we got a job after our own hearts again. A sweep was being carried out over Northern France by some bombers escorted by fighters, and the wing was to provide a covering patrol for the main formation.

We flew down to Hornchurch where the squadron had been stationed during Dunkirk, there to refuel before going over to the other side. Memories came flooding back as I led the squadron down arid came in to land on the familiar aerodrome. It looked just the same as it did seven months before. A few filled-in bomb-craters showed up from the air and the faces we saw were new.

The pilots gathered in the Watch Office talking and smoking while last-minute instructions were given and the aircraft refuelled. Then we went out on to the tarmac again to the spluttering and rumbling of engines being started up.

I climbed in and ran up the engine with more care than usual, then waved away the chocks and taxied away down the field, the other Spitfires following one by one behind me; to turn into wind and wait whilst the leading Hurricanes had taken off.

Raising one thumb I waited for the answering signal from the other section-leaders and then we were away, thundering across the green turf to rise slowly over the far hedge and climb up after the other squadrons circling the aerodrome and waiting for us.

As I got into position I called up C.O. of 249 Squadron based at North Weald. S/L Lionel Gaunce leading the Hurricanes and the wing turned south and climbed away towards the French coast.

We had instructions to patrol between Calais and Boulogne

and at 25,000 feet we turned over Cap Gris Nez and flew down the coast. Almost at once the Flak opened up at us from the Calais area, and I turned to watch the black woolly puffs of smoke blossoming lazily out just behind us, and listening for the sound of the shell exploding which would tell me that the bursts were getting too close for safety. The German batteries were putting in some quite good shooting and some of the shells seemed to be exploding very close to us although the familiar "Bop!" was inaudible.

After a few minutes the Flak stopped and we ran on down the coast only to be fired at again as we reached Boulogne. The Huns didn't seem very keen on wasting ammunition and after a few rounds ceased fire and all was quiet once more. It looked very peaceful and lovely down there in the typical French countryside with the sun shining down on the carpet of snow on the ground. They seemed to have had more of it over there than we had the other side of the Channel.

Suddenly down behind us something moving caught my eye. Looking round I saw an aircraft diving inland ten thousand feet below us. It looked like a 109 but I couldn't be sure at that distance. I wondered if he had seen us and wished I had seen him sooner—we might have been able to have got to him, but it was too late now. We shouldn't catch him this side of Paris.

As I turned over Cap Gris Nez I heard Woody's voice calling me, telling me to come home. Disappointedly I turned and flew back over the blue waters of the Channel, glistening in the afternoon sun. Blast these Huns! Where had they all got to and why wouldn't they come out and play?

Then the white cliffs of Albion slid slowly beneath the wings, and we dived away northwards towards the aerodrome.

Chapter 16

In the Pale Moonlight:
14 March 1941

Daylight activity was almost negligible now except for the odd E/A coming in under cloud coyer on days of bad weather.

Goering was concentrating all his efforts on night attacks and to help combat this day squadrons began operating during the periods of moonlight. In consequence of this increased activity by fighters, at night, the enemy's losses began to reach encouraging totals.

On March 14th, six pilots were standing by for night operations and as the sun sank in the west the thunder of engines being run up in readiness for the coming flights, reverberated across the darkening 'drome. One by one the stars came out and as the last light of the sun faded, the eastern horizon began to gleam as the moon rose slowly into the night sky.

Half an hour slowly passed and then the telephone bell rang in the Mess Hut as we sat smoking and talking.

"First two aircraft off!"

I jumped to my feet, grabbing overalls from a nearby chair, and made for the door, Arthur at my heels. As I opened the door I called over my shoulder:

"Ring the flights and tell them to start up, somebody."

Into my car and down the road to stop outside "B" Flight hut. As I got out of the car I glanced round to see where my aircraft was. The faint silhouettes of six Spitfires showed against the sky on my left and I caught sight of the little flickering stabs of flame from the exhausts of one as the fitter sat warming up the engine. That was mine.

I nipped into the flight hut to sign up for the flight, giving a hasty "Good evening," to the flight-sergeant and then out again to run to my aircraft. The fitter got out of the cockpit as I approached and stood on the wing bending down waiting to help me into the cockpit as I did up my helmet.

Catching my elbow as I pulled myself up on to the wing he helped me into the cockpit, and as I settled myself on the parachute already in the seat, passed the harness straps over my shoulders and waited whilst I clicked them home, closed the door of the cockpit.

"O.K., sir?"

"O.K., thanks," and he jumped down. Checking everything in the cockpit I waved my hand over my head and waited until the dim figures of the fitter and rigger waved an O.K. from each wing-tip, and opened the throttle. Another wave and the crew saluted and I taxied out towards the dim line of lights of the flare path to the right.

A green light came speeding down the aerodrome to rise slowly over the far boundary; the starboard navigation light of Arthur's aircraft as he took off. Glancing towards the light showing the position of the floodlight, I signalled on the identification lights for permission to take off, and as an answer flashed out, I adjusted the elevator and rudder trimmers and turned down the cockpit lights.

Peering out over the side of the cockpit, the cold blast of air from the prop brought tears to my eyes, until I had turned into position to take off, and settled back again behind the windscreen.

As I opened the throttle and eased the stick forward, the green light of the undercarriage indicator shone out dazzlingly in the dark cockpit as the throttle lever operated the automatic switch. Six seconds later the bumps of the undercarriage ceased, and we were airborne. My right hand dropped to the control lever and after a moment the green light on the instrument panel changed to red as the wheels thudded up into the wings.

Adjusting the airscrew pitch, throttling back, and closing the radiator and the cockpit hood, switching off the navigation light, I switched on the R/T and called up the ground station.

The controller answered me and I turned on to the course he gave me and began to climb up. It was a wonderful night, the midnight blue of the sky paling round the dazzling silver orb of the moon. Below the ground showed up startlingly clear, roads and fields, hedges and rivers standing out plainly visible in the moonlight. What a night for bombing!

At 15,000 feet I got instructions to circle and await further instructions. Peering down I made out the outlines of houses and streets below. A few minutes later, Woody's voice came to me over the air.

"There are several raiders in your vicinity now at your present height. Keep circling, they will pass very close to you."

"O.K., O.K."

Minutes passed, and then below me to the right I suddenly picked out the glint of something moving. As I looked, I picked out the faint form of a twin-engined aircraft flying north. Calling up the R/T I told Woody and received his acknowledgment.

Diving down I followed the aircraft and as it turned left over the city I got a perfect plan view... then, as it straightened up the glint of the moon on the wings faded and it disappeared. Frantically I turned this way and that, in an endeavour to pick up the aircraft again, but it was no good.

Suddenly brilliant flashes of flame sprang from the ground, followed a few seconds later by a cluster of flashes just below and in front of me. The guns were having a crack at the raider. Although the explosions of the shells gave me a good indication of where the E/A was, I couldn't pick him up again, and after a while fresh instructions were passed to me.

I had been up about an hour now and since there was a good head wind waiting for me on the way back, Woody decided it was time to come back. Twenty minutes later I was over the aerodrome again at 1,000 feet awaiting permission to come in to land. There were some Huns overhead and I would have to wait until they had gone, before I could have the floodlight switched on the ground. It was hardly necessary m view of the brightness of the moonlight but my landing would give away the position of the aerodrome to the E/A overhead, and they might give us a present of' a stick of bombs.

I was still circling when the controller's voice called me asking how much petrol I. had left. Pressing the button beside the gauge on the instrument panel showed me that I still had about thirty gallons left. I passed this information to the controller, and received a course to steer after one of the Huns.

Climbing up, I set course and saw above me against the dark blue of the sky the silver trail of a condensation plume. Good show! This was the answer to a night fighter's prayer. Up and up I went until I was just below the trail and then flattening out I tore along until abruptly I came to the end of it... nothing was there! The Hun had either dived down or left this particular condensation area. I judged that he was some miles ahead of me as the end of the plume looked some minutes old by the way it had thickened out. I called up the controller again and he confirmed my suspicions. The Hun was too far ahead now for me to catch him. Regretfully I turned back and dived down. A few minutes later I was circling the aerodrome again.

I flashed for permission to land and the light came back from the field. I lowered the undercart and flaps and turned in to land. As I approached the downwind hedge the floodlight came on. The moon was so bright that the light on the ground in front of me seemed almost dim, although actually it was of some thousands of candlepower and it was only as I felt the wheels bump on the ground as I flashed into the beam that I realised again how bright it really was.

Taxi-ing in I switched off and climbed out of the cockpit. As I jumped down to the ground and pushed my helmet off my ears, the fitter's voice echoed in my ear:

"Aircraft all right, sir?"

"Yes, thank you."

"Did you see anything, sir?"

"Yes, I saw one but I lost him."

"Bad luck, sir," and the man jumped up on the wing and began unscrewing the filler cap on the top tank ready for refuelling.

From the roar of the engine and slipstream I now found myself revelling in the peaceful silence of the night. The only sounds which came to my ears were the chugging of the tractor bringing the petrol tanker out to my aircraft and the faint hum high overhead of a Spitfire climbing up into the moonlit heavens to try to find the dark invaders of the night.

Lighting a cigarette I made my way to where I had parked my car and throwing my helmet and gloves into the back seat, pressed the starter and motored slowly back to the Mess hut.

The electric light had been turned out by now and in the light of two hurricane lamps I made out the dim forms of figures sprawled out in the armchairs snatching some sleep ere they were called to take off. A can of cocoa was simmering on the coal stove in the middle of the room and finding a cup I dipped it into the steaming liquid and settled myself in a chair to enjoy it. The quiet voice of Crastor in the chair next to me broke the silence.

"Did you see anything?"

"No, it's all right, you can go to sleep again."

I heard a soft chuckle and the Intelligence Officer closed his eyes.

All was peace again save for the noise of a Hun droning slowly overhead and the sound of breathing from the still forms around me.

Chapter 17

More Moonlight:
15 March 1941

The next night the Hun was active again and so were we.

Two aircraft were dispatched at a time and my turn came at eleven o'clock. It was another glorious night and as I took off I couldn't help marvelling at the beauty nature was providing and the evil use man was making of it. There is nothing in the world quite like night flying and I don't think one can fully appreciate the beauty of a moonlight night save in the air. You seem so much nearer nature herself and when the clouds cut off the silver light from the earth beneath, to climb up through the white vapour and see it shining like a white carpet below brings you into a new world, the loveliness and loneliness of which makes you catch your breath in awe. The sound of the engine and the rush of air past the cockpit fade into silence as the spell takes hold.

I was rudely awakened from my thoughts by the insistent voice of the controller asking if I was receiving him. I came back to earth as it were and switched on my transmitter. "Receiving you loud and clear, are you receiving me? over."

An affirmative came back to me and instructions for course and height, and I turned on to the given course and began to climb. Fresh instructions kept crackling in my 'phones as the controller directed me after a raider. Although I got very close to him I saw no sign of another aircraft/ and after a while I was given a new course which took me out to the north-east of the aerodrome. At 5,000 feet I cruised around following the course given to me and then circled as the controller got me in the path of an incoming raider.

"One E/A approaching you from the east at 15,000 feet."

"O.K."

Still turning I strained my eyes towards the east hoping all the while for a glimpse of a shadowy shape coming towards me, but nothing materialised. Then—

"Keep a good look out. Plots show he is right on top of you."

My heart began to beat a little faster and I found myself praying for a glimpse of that Hun. Still I saw nothing and then came the anticlimax.

"He has passed you."

I chased the invisible quarry for several minutes and then the controller called me again.

"E/A has turned away to the north. I don't think it's worth chasing him anymore. Come back and then circle."

"O.K."

As I turned east again a line of intensely white flickering light suddenly appeared miles away towards the coast—incendiaries. I watched the lights slowly turn to a steady red glow and knew that they had found a mark and had set something on fire.

The four minutes being up I circled again yawning a little as I awaited more instructions. To the north another stick of incendiaries suddenly lit up on the dark earth beneath. One by one they flickered out and the lights died. Good—those must have been on open ground.

A few seconds later a parachute flare lit up in the sky to the north-east and then another and another.

I called up on the R/T and asked if I could go and investigate, and received an O.K.

As I headed out towards the flares there came a flash and one of them disappeared. A gun had opened up from the ground and hit one, putting it out. A few seconds later came another flash and another flare went out.

In answer the Hun dropped three more and then another three. He seemed to have an unlimited quantity of the darned things!

I still did not appear to be much nearer the scene of activity and at that moment the controller called me up and told me to circle at my present position. There was another Hun coming in very close to me, and I started getting all excited again!

I think I had circled for about a minute when a stick of incendiaries appeared on the ground almost underneath me. I turned quickly and came round on a course parallel to the line of bombs. I now had a very good idea of where the Hun was, as a bomb hits the ground only a few hundred yards behind the aircraft which drops it. In addition to that I could tell what the raider's course was from the direction of the line of incendiaries.

Alas, in spite of all this I could see nothing. Then behind me to the north appeared another stick of incendiaries. Blast the fellow! He had turned right round and I yanked the kite round in a steep turn after him. It was rather like a game of blind man's buff and then to add insult to injury a stream of big white sparks whizzed past my starboard wing-tip. Tracer! The bastard was firing at me! Swearing and cursing to myself I rammed the nose down out of the way so that I could see ahead, but he wasn't there. He must have caught sight of me silhouetted against the moon.

Just then the controller's voice told me that the Hun was now a mile or two to the west of me. He must have turned round underneath me after he fired. Still feeling furious I turned west and tore after him. But no—my luck was out and when he turned away to the north, the controller called up and told me to come back and land.

A glance at the petrol-gauge confirmed his suggestion as a wise one and I turned on to the homing course he gave me and began to lose height. Corrections of the bearing were passed to me every few minutes and after a while I caught sight of the gleam of water below me and recognised the landmark. Another ten miles and as I came lower I picked up the flare-path and the aerodrome.

At a thousand feet I circled the aerodrome waiting till another Spitfire had landed. I have told earlier of an unfortunate night landing. Even in good moonlight and when conditions are favourable all the senses need to be at the alert. On this occasion, unlocking the hood I pushed it back with my elbow until it locked home in the open position. A rush of cold air filled the cockpit and I leant forward a little to get the utmost protection from the windscreen. My eyes felt tired and the night air made them water and I had to keep brushing the tears aside with my glove.

Pushing the undercarriage lever out of the top "gate," I pulled it down until it locked at the end of its travel, the red "UP" of the cockpit indicator going out to be replaced a few seconds later by a green "DOWN" as the wheels locked home in the downward position.

I throttled back as I came down the left hand side of the flare-path and as I reached the end, checked the speed on the luminous airspeed indicator and pulled down the flap lever. The aircraft slowed and the nose dropped as the flaps came down, and feeling for the rheostat control of the cockpit lights I turned it until a faint orange glow from the hooded lamp lit up the airspeed indicator and altimeter so that I could read them more easily.

110 m.p.h. I put on left bank and turned half a mile from the downwind hedge until the nose came round in line with the flare-path. The altimeter was showing 300 feet, the needle slowly moving round the dial as I lost height. I could see the hedge of the aerodrome boundary quite easily in the brilliant, moonlight. The floodlight shone out in front of me and as the hedge disappeared under the leading edge of the wing I

throttled right back and let the speed fall off to 95 m.p.h. The red light fifty yards inside the aerodrome boundary flashed past and then the airscrew lit up in a shining disc as I passed the floodlight and the beam illuminated the aircraft. A bump... pause... and then another, followed by a continuous jolting, and we were down.

One after another the lamps of the flare-path slipped by as I eased on the brakes, and as the aircraft slowed right down, turned off towards the dispersal point and taxied to where a dim figure was flashing a guiding torch to show me where to park the kite. As I neared him he came running to meet me and grabbing the wing-tip guided me in towards the chocks and pile of cockpit and engine covers marking my parking place. Braking, I gave a burst of throttle and turned the aircraft into wind and switched off, the engine spluttering until with a final kick the airscrew stopped, and all was quiet save for the whirring of the gyros behind the instrument panel.

I climbed out and answered the crew's usual enquiry about the aircraft.

"Yes—everything O.K., thanks."

Back to the flight hut to sign up after the flight that everything was in order, then a talk on the 'phone to the controller about the trip, and then back to the mess-hut for a cigarette and some cocoa, to flop down in a chair and take my ease until, perhaps, the telephone would ring and it would be my turn to go off again.

Chapter 18

Almost Like Old Times:
16 March 1941-8 April 1941

The moonlight period was over and thirty-five Huns had been knocked down in seven nights by fighters and guns. March had gone out and April had come in with a promise of spring weather. The month was eight days old and the aerodrome was basking in the noonday sun when the telephone rang in the mess-hut. This was not an unusual occurrence and I answered it without interest. Then I woke up as I heard an excited voice from the Operations Room saying that there was a "thirty plus" raid in the Channel and all aircraft were to come to "readiness" I hadn't heard those once familiar words for months now and as I passed the information over my shoulder to the rest of the pilots, their faces lit up as they leapt into activity, grabbing their flying kit and making for the door and the aircraft.

A couple of minutes later we were all ready and waiting when the order to take off came through. Three minutes afterwards 11 Spitfires were thundering across the aerodrome leaving me still wrestling with an engine which refused to start. After what seemed an age it fired, coughed, and then picked up again.

In a matter of seconds the crew had the chocks away and I opened the throttle wide and took off from where I was, racing cross wind over the green expanse of the aerodrome to rise over the far hedge and climb up towards the squadrons now wheeling high above me.

The rest of "B" Flight formed up on me after a few minutes and we climbed away towards the midday sun after "A"

Flight and the Czech squadron which was leading. They were climbing hard and I found I could make little headway on them.

It was a perfect spring morning with a visibility of at least a hundred miles. The whole of S.E. England was laid out like a map beneath us and beyond the shining ribbon of the Channel the French coast stood out clear and distinct. A broken layer of white fleecy clouds at 3,000 feet speckled the sunlit earth and blue waters of the North Sea with endless shadows. It was the sort of day when one thanks God to be alive and yet here were we, going as fast as we could in the hope of getting a chance of killing some Germans. And yet we would be cleansing the earth in so doing, that we and many millions of others might enjoy the cleanness of Nature on just such a day as this. Yes—I felt sure God had amended His commandment in our case, and I fell to thinking of the cowardly hypocrites who clung to that same commandment. "Thou shalt not kill!"—boloney! I am not of a religious nature but I have a bit of conscience, and I certainly had no regrets m killing. as many Huns as possible. Maybe it was rather a drastic way of teaching them their sorely needed lesson, but it was the only way open to us now. And with that I came back to the job in hand. We were now at 18,000 feet, almost over the Estuary with the others still about a mile ahead and a couple of thousand feet higher. As I watched the leading squadron white plumes began to form behind each aircraft to spread out into one thick woolly trail half a mile astern.

I heard Lawson call up S/L Lionel Gaunce, the English C.O. of the squadron, and draw his attention to the trail, and the Hurricanes lost height until they were clear of the condensation layer. Such blatant advertisement of our numbers and position was not conducive to a surprise attack should we meet the enemy. At last I came up just behind "A" Flight as they turned north-east off the coast to follow the other squadron of which I had now lost sight.

At that moment the controller's voice came over the R/T saying that there were some E/A to the south of us, and at the same time Lawson called up saying he had sighted some aircraft diving away below us and requesting permission to investigate. I answered with an "O.K." and flew up and down watching one or two smoke trails which were weaving about high up further out to sea. I wondered whether they were a decoy sent to try and draw us away from the shipping we were guarding in the Thames. At length the plumes turned and headed towards the land. I climbed up a little and watched until I could see the little gleaming specks of the aircraft at the head of their white tails, and as they passed overhead the sun glinted on the undersides of their wings as they banked and I saw the red, white and blue roundels at each wing-tip. O.K. They were Hurricanes.

Up and down we flew, tacking on the down sun run so that the sun was never at our tails. Minutes passed and still no formation was seen coming from the direction of the French shore.

At last the controller called up again saying that the enemy activity had dispersed and all was quite quiet again, but that we were to stay on patrol in case anything further should come in.

Every now and then another squadron of Spitfires passed us on the same patrol line and somewhere near at hand was the Czech squadron, although I couldn't see them. Twenty minutes passed and then I heard Lawson calling up the ground station. His transmission was rather faint and I wondered where he had got to and whether he had managed to find any E/A. The controller answered him and then I heard him say that he had chased some aircraft which had turned out to be Spitfires.

As I turned at one end of the patrol line I saw far away to the south-west six little white plumes standing out sharply against the deep blue of the sky. Ours or theirs I wondered. As

I watched the smoke curved round and streamed out towards the French coast. Might be ours after something but it looked rather like a small bunch of Huns going home.

I kept an eye on them out of interest more than anything else as they were much too far away to interest us, and finally saw the plumes stop as the aircraft dived down and left the condensation layer.

And all the while I was squinting into the sun and scanning the sky for a glimpse of something suspicious but nothing caught my eye. Then I heard the ground station calling L (unknown C.O. of an Hurricane squadron), telling him to come back and land. As L acknowledged the message it was passed on to Lawson and me, and I turned towards the land and began to lose height.

Down we went, although at that height only the position of the nose and the feel of the controls told that we were diving, except for the needle of the rate of climb and descent dial which was showing 2,000 feet per minute down. My ears began to sing and the noise of the engine and the rush of air past the cockpit seemed less as I began to go a little deaf with the increased pressure of the lower air.

I pushed a finger and thumb into the top of my oxygen mask and pinched my nose and blew until both ears cracked and the rush of noise came back to me. Every few thousand feet I went through the same procedure, relieving the pressure on my eardrums and restoring the normal hearing.

At four thousand feet the steady dive gradually became bumpy as we approached the top of the clouds and came into the disturbed air currents. The white masses of vapour rushed up to meet us, enveloped us, and then darkened below as the ground came into view.

The bumps had increased now as we were in the rougher air just below the clouds and the aircraft tossed about in the eddies. Automatically I corrected with the stick as first one wing and then the other dropped. The other sections of the flight closed up on me in tighter formation and I began looking round for a familiar landmark. Ah yes, that stream with the railway beside it—we were on our course, and I began peering ahead for a glimpse of the bunch of trees just south of the aerodrome. After a minute I picked it out and turned slightly until the nose of my kite was pointing at it. At the same time half a mile to the right 12 Hurricanes emerged from the clouds above, diving towards the aerodrome now visible ahead.

At a thousand feet we roared across the green expanse and turned left round the circuit. Switching on the R/T I called the ground station and told him I was now over base and then told the other section leaders to break away and land individually with their own sections. Then I came in and landed, to be followed in quick succession by the rest of the flight and finally by "A" Flight, who had by now almost reached the aerodrome.

I taxied in, waved away the other aircraft in my section, each to his individual dispersal point. I switched off, climbed out and walked to the flight hut to sign up for the flight, and to light a cigarette whilst the others came in.

Then back to the Mess for a welcome drink before lunch. There might be better luck for us this afternoon.

Conclusion

And now as I sit penning the last of this book, the sun is streaming through the window, lighting a vivid pattern on the paper before me. Glancing back through the chapters I realise what fun it has been writing them and reliving those fights over the sunlit coast of Belgium and the lovely countryside of Kent. I have tried to take you up high into the blue with me to meet the Luftwaffe and to give you an idea of what it's like up there. I hope I have succeeded.

I am no "ace" and I know of many who could tell you a far far better tale than I, beside whose experiences mine are nothing. It isn't too easy writing a book in these times. Time is the great enemy, and I have had to write in spare moments between flights and after the squadron has been released in the evening.

Mine is only one side of the picture, the easiest side, I think. Compare it with that of the bomber boys—perhaps one day their story will be recorded by one of them, and that will be a book worth reading.

But before I put my pen down for the last time I want you to think of the lads who are, so to speak, behind the scenes, the fitters and riggers, the engineer officers, the flight-sergeants (the backbone of the Service), the Controllers in the Operations Room, and all the other ground personnel who make it possible for the pilots to do their job. Working in the background, no glamour, no "gongs," just getting on with it. So to them I say, "Thank you." The spring of another year of war has come. Hitler has walked into Jugoslavia—well, some of the way, anyway—and his forces have reached the Egyptian border. Perhaps he thinks he's winning—well, perhaps he does, they say he's mad, anyway! But the day of reckoning will come, come what may, and then will follow the task of making Germany fit to exist in a civilised world. Some task, but we will do it and— Just a moment, the telephone has rung... "Hello... Operations?... Yes... Yes, speaking. Thirty plus over the Channel? Good show... Do you want us off right away?... O.K., cheerio."

"O.K., boys, we're off. Somebody tell the flight."

Sorry—I must go now—I can't write more.

Where the hell's my "Mae West?"—Ah, I've got it— I wonder if this is the beginning of another Blitz—invasion, maybe— well, let 'em all come—the more the merrier—so long!

List of Illustrations

Unless otherwise indicated all illustrations are courtesy of Dilip Sarkar.

Spitfire!

44. Sgt Jennings, Author, "Flash," "Grumpy," F/Lt. McPhie., "Rangy", S/L. Burton, Brinsden (on wing), and Leckrone. 45. Spitfires on night patrol. 46. 'Scramble'. From the alert relayed from a fighter station to the airfields fighters could be in the air within minutes. From the Battle of Britain Monument (Victoria embankment, London) sculptured by Paul Day. Photo © Jonathan Reeve. 47. Pilots scramble to their Spitfires, June 1940. © Jonathan Reeve JR1631b83p234T 19391945. 48. A fighter pilot springs into action when the order comes, 1940. © Jonathan Reeve JR1625b82p63B 19391945. 49. Spitfires on patrol, 1940. © Jonathan Reeve JR1624b82p62-3T 19391945. 50. Hurricanes pulling away after making contact with German aircraft. © Jonathan Reeve JR1209b71pic9 19391945. 51. A fighter pilot with R/T equipment. From the Battle of Britain Monument (Victoria embankment, London) sculptured by Paul Day. Photo © Jonathan Reeve. 52. Air combat, a Spitfire pilot trying to avoid cannon shells fired from an ME 109 on his tail. From the Battle of Britain Monument (Victoria embankment, London) sculptured by Paul Day. Photo © Jonathan Reeve. 53. & 54. British gun-camera images of German aircraft being shot down. © Jonathan Reeve JR1215b69pic70 19391945, © Jonathan Reeve JR1451b79p33 19391945. 55. The Battle of Britain was very visible to the British from the ground with swirling vapour trails marking the dogfights in the summer skies of 1940. © Jonathan Reeve JR1630b82p84T 19391945. 56. A doomed German Dornier 17 bomber aircraft plummeting earthwards after being attacked by British fighters. © Jonathan Reeve JR1449b79p31 19391945. 57. A downed Me 109. This was the Luftwaffe's main fighter. © Jonathan Reeve JR1211b71pic18 19391945. 58. A downed He 111. © Jonathan Reeve JR1212b71pic20 19391945. 59. The young Brian John Edward Lane, whilst growing up in Pinner, Middlesex. 60. Pilot Officer Brian Lane pictured whilst flying Gloster Gauntlet biplane fighters with either 66 or 213 Squadrons before the Second World War. 61. A formal studio portrait taken at the time of Brian Lane's DFC was awarded for his leadership of 19 Squadron during the Dunkirk air-fighting - after the Commanding Officer, Squadron Leader Geoffrey Stephenson, had been shot down and captured during the Squadron's first engagement. 62. Flight Lieutenant Brian Lane pictured with his famous wife, the glamorous motor-racing champion Eileen Ellison. 63. An officer and a gentleman: Brian Lane in civilian clothes. 64. Squadron Leader Brian Lane, posing in flying helmet and oxygen mask, whilst serving briefly in the Western Desert in 1942. 65. Squadron Leader Brian Lane whilst serving at RAF Middle East HQ in 1942. Unfortunately Lane was unsuited to the climate and posted home in June 1942. Six months later he was reported missing in action whilst leading a completely useless sortie over the Dutch coast.

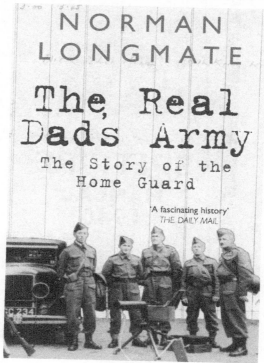

Also available from Amberley Publishing

How to fly the legendary fighter plane in combat using the manuals and instructions supplied by the RAF during the Second World War

Also available from Amberley Publishing

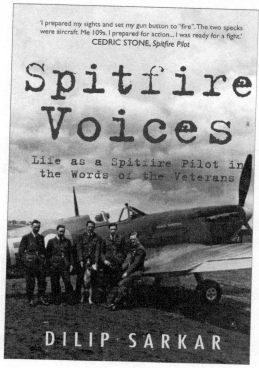

'I prepared my sights and set my gun button to "fire". The two specks were aircraft. Me 109s. I prepared for action... I was ready for a fight.' CEDRIC STONE, *Spitfire Pilot*

Spitfire Voices

Life as a Spitfire Pilot in the Words of the Veterans

DILIP SARKAR

Spitfire fighter pilots tell their extraordinary stories of combat during the Second World War

'I prepared my sights and set my gun button to "fire". The two specks were aircraft. Me 109s. I prepared for action… I was ready for a fight.' CEDRIC STONE, Spitfire Pilot

'There is nothing glamorous in being a fighter pilot. There is nothing glamorous in killing and being killed. Exciting, very exciting, sometimes too exciting, but definitely not glamorous, not even in a Spitfire.' MAURICE MACEY, Spitfire Pilot

£20 Hardback
169 Photographs
360 pages
978-1-4456-0042-0

Available from all good bookshops or to order direct
Please call **01453-847-800**
www.amberleybooks.com

Also available from Amberley Publishing

18 Spitfire and Hurricane fighter pilots recount their experiences of combat during the Battle of Britain

'Dilip knows more about me and the pilots with whom I flew during the Battle of Britain than we do! If anyone ever needs to know anything about the RAF during the summer of 1940, don't ask the Few, ask him!' GEORGE 'GRUMPY' UNWIN, Battle of Britain fighter ace

£9.99 Paperback
55 Photographs
224 pages
978-1-4456-0282-0

Available from all good bookshops or to order direct
Please call **01453–847–800**
www.amberleybooks.com

Also available from Amberley Publishing

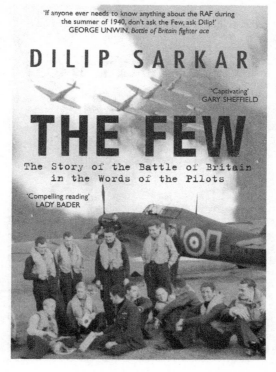

'If anyone ever needs to know anything about the RAF during the summer of 1940, don't ask the Few, ask Dilip!'
GEORGE UNWIN, *Battle of Britain fighter ace*

DILIP SARKAR

'Captivating'
GARY SHEFFIELD

THE FEW

The Story of the Battle of Britain in the Words of the Pilots

'Compelling reading'
LADY BADER

The history of the Battle of Britain in the words of the pilots

'Over the last 30 years Dilip Sarkar has sought out and interviewed or corresponded with numerous survivors worldwide. Many of these were not famous combatants, but those who formed the unsung backbone of Fighter Command in 1940. Without Dilip's patient recording and collation of their memories, these survivors would not have left behind a permanent record.' LADY BADER
'A well-researched detailed chronicle of the Battle of Britain'. HUGH SEBAG MONTEFIORE

£14.99 Paperback
129 photographs
320 pages
978-1-4456-0050-5

Available from all good bookshops or to order direct
Please call **01453-847-800**
www.amberleybooks.com

Also available from Amberley Publishing

The amazing story of one of the 'Few', fighter ace Tom Neil who shot down 13 enemy aircraft during the Battle of Britain

'A thrilling new book...Tom Neil is one of the last surviving heroes who fought the Luftwaffe'
THE DAILY EXPRESS

'The best book on the Battle of Britain' SIR JOHN GRANDY, Marshal of the RAF

This is a fighter pilot's story of eight memorable months from May to December 1940. By the end of the year he had shot down 13 enemy aircraft, seen many of his friends killed, injured or burned, and was himself a wary and accomplished fighter pilot.

£20 Hardback
120 Photographs (20 colour)
320 pages
978-1-84868-848-3

Available from all good bookshops or to order direct
Please call **01453-847-800**
www.amberleybooks.com

Also available from Amberley Publishing

'A poignant and evocative account of what it felt like to be a young fighter pilot in the Battle of Britain'
JULIA GREGSON, *bestselling author & daughter of Barry Sutton*

Fighter Boy
Life as a Battle of Britain Pilot

BARRY SUTTON

The Battle of Britain memoir of Hurricane pilot Barry Sutton, DFC

At 23 years of age, Barry Sutton had experienced more than the average person experiences in a lifetime. This book, based on a diary he kept during the war, covers September 1939 to September 1940 when he was shot down and badly burned.

£20 Hardback
20 illustrations
224 pages
978-1-84868-849-0

Available from all good bookshops or to order direct
Please call **01453-847-800**
www.amberleybooks.com

Also available from Amberley Publishing

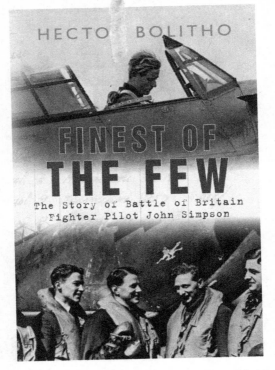

The remarkable Battle of Britain experiences of fighter pilot John Simpson, DFC

Written by 43 Squadron's intelligence officer, Hector Bolitho, Finest of the Few revolves around Bolitho's friend, fighter ace John W. C. Simpson, who shot down 13 German aircraft during the Battle of Britain. The book was written in 1941 and was based on John Simpson's Combat Reports, his personal letters and papers together with Hector's own recollections of the heady days of the summer of 1940.

£20 Hardback
80 photographs
256 pages
978-1-4456-0057-4

Available from all good bookshops or to order direct
Please call **01453-847-800**
www.amberleybooks.com